GYPSY SONGMAN

BY

JERRY JEFF WALKER

Woodford Press

Printed in the United States.

Book design: Mark Shepard.

Cover design: Jim Santore.

Illustrations by Ben Jennings.

Library of Congress Catalog Card Number 99-65702
ISBN: 0-942627-57-1

Distributed in the United States and Canada by Andrews McMeel Publishing, Kansas City, MO

Woodford Press
5900 Hollis Street, Suite K
Emeryville, CA 94608

C. David Burgin, Editor and Publisher
Daniel C. Ross, CEO and Publisher
William F. Duane, Senior Vice President
Anne Crump, Promotion Director

Associate Publishers:
Franklin M. Dumm
William W. Scott, Esq.
William B. McGuire, Esq.

Contents

To Jessie Jane and Django Walker, my heroes.

Special Thanks

Phillip Finch for his editorial hand and telephone ear.
John T. Davis for his criticism and wit.

And especially Walter Gibson for his patience and tireless retyping of the text.

And Earl Casey . . .
How to thank Earl?
I asked him.

Dear Jerry Jeff:

In the acknowledgments, would you consider some wording which refers to me in some manner beyond building the chronology?

Every word of this book you have either written, edited or otherwise approved. It is yours, every word, and the entire style, all touched by your hand.

Other than a chronology, I would like to think I contributed belief. I know your story is a great story, a grand story of life and living. I think of what you said once: "I don't care how they make the wine. I care what they do when they drink it."

Something like that, maybe?

I used to make wine. Picked the grapes in the backyard, tried to keep the goats out of them. Made wine, really awful wine, which I drank with great ceremony and offered to horrified friends. I really cared how the wine was made, but what I remember now is the friends I made, many of them yours.

During this last decade, my red truck made it 250,000 miles, much of it between Austin and Atlanta and back. I lived a summer writing at the Heart of Texas Motel, drinking Shiner for breakfast and wondering what color poodle made that piss spot in the rug.

I ran down your girlfriends in the Oklahoma prairie. Met and drank with your friends as friends of mine. I fell in love with a Mexican girl, who left me for a cold old man who was just a wee bit crazier than she was. And I spent one magic evening in a bar somewhere in Colorado with you, a guitar, your pilot and a couple of cases of beer, watching blue bolt lightning tease the mountains, feeling forever young.

Give me one sentence of that, please. Maybe the line about making the wine.

Earl

Foreword

By Bud Shrake

There was a period during Jerry Jeff's career when many people came to his live shows for two main reasons — to hear him sing his classic, "Mr. Bojangles," and to see if he might tumble off the stage and hurt himself. He was sort of a theatrical NASCAR race, an act that was full of thrills and suspense. We became friends during this period, in 1973, at the Luckenbach World's Fair, and I hung out with him and his Lost Gonzo Band until my doctor made me stop.

And now look at old Scamp Walker. Instead of being in his grave, as anyone who knew him long ago would have expected, Jerry Jeff is in his prime, a favorite from the White House to the waffle shop. His concerts are packed with high school kids as well as with adult crowds that span economic and political chasms. They all have one thing in common: they love Jerry Jeff.

They whoop when he is rowdy and they grow misty when he does one of his soul songs. They fill the Paramount Theatre in Austin every year for his birthday party. They follow him to his getaway on the beach in Belize. They flock to see him in New York or Aspen or London. And in truth, Jerry Jeff is performing better than ever, with more authentic, nonchemically induced gusto, in control of his talent now in his wiser years.

He is no longer a threat to fall through the drums, but his act still carries an edge of menace that appeals to his fans who are never sure exactly what their maverick hero might say or do next. So why didn't he die like he was supposed to?

In my opinion, Jerry Jeff is alive and flourishing today — financially successful and even healthy — because a singular Austin girl named Susan Streit selected him out of the herd of her suitors, married him and set the two of them on the often turbulent road that has turned Jerry Jeff into a big business as well as a cult hero.

The beautiful Susan turned out to have a hard head for numbers and a powerful personality. She gets what she wants, and one thing she wants is for her husband to thrive.

He does his own music in his own way. If he desires to make an album sitting by the edge of the ocean, that is what will happen — and when a fan buys the album through the catalog or over the Internet, the album is bought from Jerry Jeff and Susan and their company, not from a mogul in Los Angeles or Nashville. Jerry Jeff is a troubadour with a big database.

The Gonzos are a remarkable group of musicians, all the more so because they have stayed with Jerry Jeff through the wars, defeats and triumphs of the last two and a half decades. They are stars in their own right. I used to think several of them would break from the band and become famous individually — a couple have done it, with varying success — but watching the Gonzos perform at Jerry Jeff's fifty-seventh birthday party concert, it occurred to me how youthful they all still look, and how they have nurtured each other all these years and fed off the spirit of their resident megalomaniac, Jerry Jeff. They belong together, that's all. They are in the same karass.

A few years ago when Jerry Jeff started talking about writing his autobiography, I thought this would provide employment for at least a dozen researchers, because the author could not possibly recall much of his twenties, thirties and forties. But his memory proves surprising, and he has gone back and interviewed persons from his past, including the cops who arrested him in New Orleans and threw him into the cell where he met Mr. Bojangles.

Back in the late '70s, Jerry Jeff and I were in Denver in the middle of the night playing a game at the house of some show business guy. The game was that you stood with your back against the wall and tossed a quarter at an upturned hat that lay on the living room floor two doors away down the hall. Jerry Jeff and I beat the host and his friends out of enough money that they complained when we said we were leaving, and accused us of taking advantage of them

Jerry Jeff made them an offer. He would try one last throw — imagine, now, how difficult it is to throw a quarter into a hat fully two rooms away — and if he landed the coin inside the hat, we would give them their money back. If he missed, we were leaving, no hard feelings.

The host thought that was a lousy offer, but it was the only offer, so he and his friends took it. Jerry Jeff leaned against the wall, squinted at that distant hat — and threw the quarter like a line drive straight inside the crown.

We left without their money. Jerry Jeff had made one of the great throws in the history of this particular game, just so we could give their money back. I won't try to analyze this story, but to me it has always illustrated the strength and the capriciousness of Jerry Jeff, not to mention the talent and showmanship.

Gypsy Songman will reveal the qualities I am talking about.

Bud Shrake
Austin, Texas, 1999

Introduction

For years I've thought I'd tell the tale
of how a small-town boy leaves the snowdrifts of upstate New York
and finds magic and adventure
on the highways of America.
With no plan in mind
but the joy of the open road
and a song to sing
I wound up playing music all my life.
While traveling around I thought
"I'll gather up some songs from people I meet,
and later in life I'll sit around
and tell a few tales about those people
and play their songs."
Basically, that's what I do for a living.
Now the telling of that tale
starts with a letter…

Dear Mr. Walker:

A week or so ago you were in a small town in Louisiana which happens to be the home of my kids, a city I loved in and worked in for a *long* time. I flew from Atlanta on a quick weekend dash to see you perform. You were playing Enoch's, a funky little crawfish joint jammed with maybe a hundred folks packed knee to knee.

When you walked through the sad screen door of that place, my heart fell to see you alone. My lord, the man's ruined, abandoned by backup, picking for the pass of a hat.

And then this fellow began to play.

I'd seen Jerry Jeff many times before. The lovers always have. But I had never seen him alone before. He was . . .

Well, let me tell you how he was. An accomplished solo singer and picker. His voice, the same one I've hollered to the moon with many times.

Here I am, pushing forty, on my last breath at times, flying 500 miles to get a glimpse of someone and something that means something to me. And this guy comes through the front door of a nowhere joint in somewhere, Louisiana, and makes it come alive again.

Casual as the last kiss, playing to himself with relish.

So the rest of us sang along, as usual.

In the lines outside your concerts, people tell stories about you. Guess you miss that part of it. Yeah, well there was the time that . . . And once I saw him when he   And

Magnolia, Mississippi, with narcs in the honeysuckle

Outlaw Festival June 28, 1976, almost died the next day

Michigan, where you said goodbye 'fore you said hello

The Summit, Houston

Atlanta, by many names

In the eyes of my best friend

And then, let me tell you about this, there was the time he came into this nowhere bar in somewhere Louisiana and played like none of us was ever gonna die, and when we did, he'd be there too. Mighty fine evening, Mr. Walker.

Earl Casey

My reply . . .

Dear Earl:

I just got around to rereading your letter and thought this might be the right time to reflect. First time I read it, I was lying here recuperating from back surgery, and had just gotten a call from Tony Drago, my old high school basketball coach, who knew me when I was Ronald Clyde Crosby. There was going to be a reunion in Oneonta, New York, for our class. Thirty years.

All those years on the move . . .

Name changes . . .

Finding myself . . .

Broken nose, broken fingers, broken foot . . .

Broken guitars . . .

Broken promises . . .

Broken back . . .

Now is the time to mend.

Any honest life story is going to be about mistakes as well as successes, and I've had plenty of both. You can't rehearse life — you have to live it.

Some of the best things that ever happened to me came my way because I was willing to cut loose. I was a street singer in New Orleans when I was busted for standing on a table-top in the French Quarter and serenading a young lovely whose name I never knew. It cost me a weekend in jail, sharing a cell with an old street singer who told me about his life. A few years later I wrote a song about him: "Mr. Bojangles" launched my career.

I could always wing it; in fact, the looser things were, the more I shined.

Ramblin' scramblin'.

But by the late '70s, Jerry Jeff Walker was rolling out of control. Jerry Jeff was bigger and wilder than Ron Crosby from Oneonta, New York, could ever have imagined.

I'd been running away since my sixteenth summer. Ran away from home, ran away from small town life, ran away from the Army, ran away from my family and my name.

Now, I was thirty-six years old, bloated, overweight, smoking too much, eating too lit-tle, consuming a fifth of whiskey and a couple of grams of coke a day. More or less sleep-ing in a car, waking up outside lawyer's offices and honky-tonks. Wearing polyester so the wrinkles wouldn't show.

About twenty years back, I had written a great little song. Now, there were fifteen albums. Played about 200 shows a year with eight or ten people traveling, sometimes in private planes. I was the wandering father of a baby daughter, and my wife was talking about divorce. A few million bucks had come and gone. The IRS was after me for $150,000 in back taxes and threatening possible charges of defrauding the government. In six weeks, I had run up $90,000 on my credit card, and American Express was suing to get it back.

While putting out these fires I was trying to sever a ten-year relationship with my busi-ness manager and finish my last album for Elektra records. Not a happy mix.

There's a story herein how a young kid from Oneonta, New York, hitchhiked his way into that mess. And another story in how I got from there to where you found me playing solo in that ramshackle joint in Louisiana, and another in how I got from that joint to play-ing a presidential inaugural ball.

A lot of stories. And when you have the time, Earl, I'll be glad to tell them all.

Jerry Jeff Walker

Chapter 1

What's in a name . . . The freedom of a small town . . . The first guitar . . . And then came rock and roll . . . Spring break and making the break . . .

Some of the names I've been known by over the years:

Ronald Clyde Crosby
Jerry Ferris
Jeff Walker
Jerry Jeff Walker
Scamp Walker
Jacky Jack
Jacky Jack Double Trouble
J.J. Snowdrift

The first time, I was born Ronald Clyde Crosby, son of Mel and Alma Crosby, high school sweethearts. March 16, 1942. After the war, with Dad out of the Army, he and the G.I. Bill bought a house on East End Avenue in Oneonta. Monthly payment thirty-five dollars, and to swing it, Mel and Alma both had to work hard. For years my father held down two jobs, refereeing basketball and soccer, and tending bar.

Oneonta had once been a railroad boomtown, and you could still see traces of the old prosperity in the wide sidewalks and big front porches.

It was an Ozzie and Harriet life for me. Tuna sandwich and Oreo cookies after school. Crewcut boys riding thick-tired bicycles with old playing cards chattering in the spokes. Shooting hoops in the backyard until dark. I had free run of the neighborhood. No fences between the neighbors' back yards. So it was one big playground.

The wistful bright colors of a happy childhood.

Kids all walked to school. The elementary school

Playing cowboy in Oneonta, New York, circa 1948: "Nobody moves, nobody gets hurt" . . . just another young desperado, waitin' for a choo-choo.

The picture of innocence in first grade in Oneonta, New York.

was about six blocks from our homes. We made a little line each day. Little ants going back and forth.

East End Avenue and the fields around it were our own private world. My best friend, Mike Patton, lived two streets over. East End Avenue was the last street in that end of town. There was a big field right beside the street and it was all ours. We built forts, showed our private parts, played tag until we dropped. You could hear a lot of the after-school music of the calling voices of children. Boys playing games in the fields. Dividing into teams for a game of baseball. An old coffee can was second base, the edge of a shed was third.

And then, around six o'clock, the voices of mothers began chirping from front porches and back doors. One seemed to trigger the rest, like dogs howling at a siren.

"Ronnie. Ronnie. Suppertime. Time to come home."

About the same time from another house, "Anthony!"

"Sammy. Samm-eeeee."

The neighborhood. Not much happening. Just life its ownself. Living in a small town and enjoying the freedom to ride a bicycle or walk home down safe streets.

Enjoying the freedom. Freedom to do nothing if you want. Explore your own imagination. And have the time to do that. Children from small towns with unlocked doors are more naturally open to everything around them.

Weekends, summers, I spent on the farm with my mother's parents, Clyde and Jessie Conrow. It was a small dairy farm, sixteen cows, a garden, self-sufficient. It reached like a morning-yawn stretch from the high meadow, down the slopes, past the pond to the flat broad bottomland beside the river.

Clyde Conrow was my first hero. A big man. Wire-rimmed glasses, broad potbelly. Arms and hands strong from years of muscling hay bales and pitchforks and tractors and fence posts.

Clyde relished life, and he taught me to do the same. He loved Sunday dinners, having us all together around a dinner table at a picture window that overlooked the fields. Chicken and dumplings, a big spread, fresh-baked bread and home-churned butter and homemade ice cream.

After dinner we would all sing songs while Grandma Jessie played the piano — everybody sang.

The Conrows had a family band that often played at farmers' dances in the area.

Clyde played the drums and called square dances. Jessie played the piano. The sisters, Alma and Norma, were singers. Often they would hire a pickup player or two: a banjo, rhythm guitar, maybe a trumpet or a sax if the dance was big enough.

Sometimes, if the dance went late, they'd roll in just in time to start chores. Clyde would haul the drum set out of the car and into the farmhouse, then head straight for the barn where the cows waited for those thick-fingered hands.

I grew up surrounded by music. Mel and Alma had been local dance champs, 1939. Alma and Aunt Norma and a friend had a singing group, the Southside Trio, later the Three Queens of Melody. Norma played piano professionally in some of the nicer clubs around the area, and belonged to a jazz group with a popular radio show. Grandma Jessie had played the piano since she was a child. She could not pass a piano without stopping to caress the keys "to see what they have to say."

When I was in junior high school, my family moved to Maple Street in the middle of town. An apartment. I made a bedroom up in the attic. It became my lair, where I spent hours listening to my mom and dad's records — in 1954, most kids didn't own their own stereos. Frank Sinatra, Mills Brothers, Ella Fitzgerald, Louis Armstrong, Benny Goodman and Chet Baker.

A tenant downstairs from our apartment owned a Harmony guitar that he could never master. I started borrowing it, exploring its sound, haltingly learning to play. That Christmas, Grandma Jessie bought that guitar from him for eighty dollars. There it was that one special morning, leaning against the tree, a bright ribbon swathed around it. The first guitar.

The Gift

In a boarding house, I'd lay upstairs and dream of how I'd live someday
Downstairs there sat a man who had a guitar he'd never learned to play.
For my thirteenth birthday Grandma bought the guitar
Told me I should learn how to play
And the gift she gave me changed me
'Cause the music is the main thing that's got me to this point here today.

CHORUS:
    And I was lucky, 'cause I used her gift
    To get in touch with how to live
    And looking back I now realize
    Music changed my life
    Yes, music filled a void in my life.

I began to hang around a pizza joint downtown where neighborhood kids too young for bars and nightlife would talk and sing along with the jukebox.

Jim Mosca owned the pizza parlor. He was a big, lumbering man, a retired locomotive engineer from the days of coal-fired trains. He played guitar and sang beautifully. And he cared about kids. Mosca listened to my early attempts at the guitar. He found me a ukulele — much easier to play — and taught me a few chords.

Here's a picture from the past: my buddy Mike Patton at the wheel of his '55 Chevy,

My inspiration — Grandma Jessie, a k a Conrow, in Oneonta, New York, sometime in the 1970s. Jessie bought me my first guitar. She used to say, "I never walk past the piano when I don't sit down for at least a moment and see what it says." Spoken like a true musician.

driving down the streets of Oneonta. Me riding shotgun, plunking away on the ukulele singing "Up A Lazy River," top of my lungs.

Then came rock and roll.

Then came real life.

A game room for teenagers opened near the center of town.

Pool table, ping-pong, music in the back room. A hangout. Friday and Saturday nights, it echoed with the racket of teenagers, shouting and running from one end to the other. And the same walk that can take me ten blocks downtown in the morning to school can take me ten blocks downtown into the nights of Oneonta, college town. When school was in session, Oneonta State and Hartwick College had a combined population as large as the town itself.

"Mom, I'm just gonna walk downtown and see what's going on."

And I became a rascal.

My memories from those years are of basketball, music and girls.

By the time I was fifteen, I was tall and lanky and had some street smarts. I blended in with older kids, a loner who hung out with other loners. Some were in college at Oneonta State, some couldn't even spell it. Most were already losers of a sort.

A couple of them had cars. We'd head up to the college campus, meet some girls, take 'em parking.

Sports became the center of my high school life. I could play — baseball, basketball. Especially basketball. Oneonta High always had winning teams when I was there.

Every team I played on would have a winning season, especially basketball. By that time, I'd been on the basketball team since the seventh grade.

I was popular, athletic, and I had lousy study habits.

But I did love to read.

In class, when I wasn't staring out the window, I'd be paging through Thoreau, Camus, Emerson.

Planting the seeds.

A lot of this love of books came from Charlie Galvin, Aunt Norma's husband. Alcoholic, insomniac, jazz sax player, genius, ravenous reader.

Uncle Charlie presided from a lounge chair in his living room, a shiny leatherette recliner surrounded by piles and boxes of books. Afternoons, he would go out to buy a pint at the liquor store. On his way home, he dropped by the drug store and spun the book rack. Pulling off books as it was whirling.

Didn't matter what he picked. By the end of the week, he'd have read everything in the rack.

He left piles of empty bottles, and boxes upon boxes of books. I would dive into the books, picking through cheapo dime novels, falling into a pile of Thoreau.

What was left of my childhood ended on a sultry day when I was fifteen.

The prodigal son returns. Playing in Oneonta, New York, with my mother, Alma, in the foreground.

That one last summer.

When I was twelve, I had started to caddy at the local golf course, and I'd missed a few summers on the farm. One day Clyde tweaked me: "Guess you don't love your grandpa anymore, you don't come down to the farm to see me as much as you used to."

So I went to work for Clyde that summer with my running buddy, Mike Patton, putting away hay.

Since we did a man's work, we were allowed to sit with the men and have one beer after the chores. Just one. There, in the frigid water of a spring house, were a few bottles of Ballantine beer, waiting for the end of the day. Mike and I felt like men.

Then, that August evening.

We were on our third and final load of the day, with the sun going down. Mike Patton swung the last bale to the top of the wagon, climbed on the back. Clyde pulled the wagon with a tractor. I was going to follow in a Jeep.

As I checked the gate, I glanced back to see Clyde and the tractor and the wagon chugging over the hill.

So I never saw it happen. On the steep far side of the hill, with the weight of the hay wagon behind it, the tractor began to slide, brakes grabbing, wheels locking.

I drove over the hill to find the tractor in a ditch, its right rear wheel still spinning. The hay wagon was jackknifed, Mike thrown a good twenty yards away but unhurt.

Clyde was pinned beneath the tractor. He just lay there, so still.

Mike and I were frightened kids, panicked, crying. We couldn't lift the tractor.

But it didn't matter. Clyde had died almost instantly when his head hit a single large, flat rock that sat in the field.

After the ambulance left, I disappeared, ran off to the high meadow that had always been my favorite place to spend time with Clyde. It had lush grass, had strawberries and blueberries. A quiet place, far from the road.

I sat there now in the darkness, salt tears stinging my eyes, going crazy, realizing that some things broken can't be mended.

It's over.

Just gone.

Rollin' Wheels

As a young boy
I helped the old man, working
I helped the old man, working in the field
and every day, we hauled the hay
to the rolling of the wheels
till one day, tractor lay the old man
down to the ground
tractor pitched him into a ditch
and left dusty sound
of the wheel that kept spinnin' round
wheel kept spinnin' round
Rolling wheels

rollin' on
taking us all on our way
rolling wheels
rollin' on
takin' back all that they gave
takin' us all on our way
takin' back all that they save
takin' us all on our way

*   *   *

If I had never become Jerry Jeff Walker, they would still remember me in Oneonta as Ron Crosby, starting forward on the town's championship high school basketball team. By the time I was in junior high, I lived to play basketball. In the winter I would shovel the snow off the outdoor court so that I could shoot. On Saturdays, my buddies and I would sneak into unlocked school gyms until a janitor chased us off. I would play pickup games and in the senior leagues.

Sometime around 1954: in the fields with Grandpa Clyde, with Jinks and James. It's a vanished world.

My junior year, the varsity went 16-3. My senior year, won a state championship and beat everybody who would play us.

Otherwise, Ron Crosby at age seventeen made for a bleak picture.

Rebellion. Out of control. Hormones running wild. Cigarette posing. I loved to dance and hang out. I looked older than my age, old enough to buy a beer. And I did.

Sometimes I was late coming home, sometimes I wouldn't come home at all. When my father tried to enforce a nine o'clock curfew, I moved out and into Mike Patton's house.

After three weeks, my parents and I called a truce. I agreed to finish high school, living at home. It seemed that things were going better. Graduation was scheduled for June of 1960. After that I would be on my own.

11

By now it had dawned on me that I wasn't going to college. This meant that after graduation, I would be headed out of Oneonta for good.

Everybody my age was headed out of Oneonta for good.

Once Oneonta had been a rail center of the East Coast, home of a huge switching yard and the largest roundhouse in the world. But that world was changing and the railroads weren't what they had been. The last passenger train passed through town in 1954, taking the town's future along with it, and by 1960 there was nothing to hold me there once I had kept my promise to my parents.

June, I would be out of there. That was the plan.

In the final weeks of my senior year, I realized that I didn't have enough credited hours to get out of school if I didn't pass every course in my last semester. I gave it a good push, but chemistry got me. I ended half a credit short of graduation. Seemed unfair to me. I had never missed a class in four years. I had sung four years of choir and traveled to contests, but got no credit.

So much for school shit, I thought.

The school allowed me to go through all the graduation exercises. But in the summer of 1960, I had to make up that one half credit. I had promised my folks I would graduate, so I stayed for summer school.

Just a couple more months, that's all.

But that was a story which had trapped many before me. Just stick around a little while longer . . .

Somehow, the fall of 1960 found me still in Oneonta. I was out of my parents' home, sleeping on the couch in my Grandmother Jessie's trailer, usually after drinking beer way past closing time. I made a polite point to be on the couch by dawn, when she would be up, busily hustling around the trailer and charging out the door into the day. She would pour coffee and see me lying there, figuring I'd been there all night. Most mornings after she left, I would just stay on the couch until after noon, resting up for another night of gettin' drunk a lot and staying out late.

There wasn't anything I wanted to work at.

And then Mel saw me one day lying there limp on the couch. Looked at me with rough, direct, penetrating eyes.

"Ron, you're gonna lay around and be a bum and you're gonna break your mother's heart. And you're gonna break mine. If you don't wanna go to school, you gotta get a job, you gotta do something. You can't do *nothin'*. Son, if nothing else, why don't ya join the National Guard? Get some of your military obligation out of the way."

Mel, platoon sergeant for the Oneonta Guard detachment for years. Standing over me, his guilty son.

"Get on with it," the moment seemed to say.

So I did. Got a job delivering Ballantine beer five days a week. Joined the New York National Guard. In the spring of '61, I went to Fort Dix for basic training. Because I'd had some training in our unit in Oneonta, they made me squad leader during basic.

So here I was, PFC Ron Crosby. Tailored uniform, leader of men.

I knew the drills, knew commands, wearing a private's stripes but acting as a corporal. A platoon would face left and step off to my barked order. I loved to sing "cadence" as we marched along.

On leave, the trainees would go off post to drink in those ever-present bars near military bases. I was nineteen years old, but at the time New Jersey's drinking age was twenty-one. The other guys and I dressed up one night, ready to hit the streets.

"I'm not old enough to drink in New Jersey," I told 'em.

One guy's hand went into his wallet. He came up with several pieces of identification, peeled off a draft card, handed it to me and waved me out the door.

The name on the card was "Jerry Ferris." I kept the ID, and Jerry Ferris later became my first alias on the road.

When I got back to Oneonta after basic training, I discovered that the Guard had become another trap. I couldn't be transferred to another unit in another town unless I had a job and an address. So I worked for Ballantine and hung out in town checking out the locals. Tough time for my parents watching me flounder. I even got arrested for DWI on the New York Thruway, going to Long Island one weekend.

The town was smothering me. I knew that my future lay beyond those dusty hills.

I rented an apartment with a pal named Danny Brown, and started hanging out with a bunch of guys five or six years older than I was. Some had been off to college. Others had fought in the Korean War. All had returned to Oneonta and gotten stuck there. We'd stay up late, talk, listen to LPs of jazz and hip comedians. Chet Baker, Miles Davis. Brother Dave, Lenny Bruce, Lord Buckley.

One of my buddies was Silky Sullivan, a young teacher, wise and learned and well-read. Silky lived in a loft apartment with stacks of books and records and not much else. On slow nights in the bars he would sit reciting haiku.

Silky and I and the others would talk constantly of road trips. Go out to California, maybe get some work. See what was happening outside Oneonta.

And then it was not just talk. Danny Brown and Nicky Lambros headed off to Las Vegas with a girl. Steve Crounse drove down to Florida for the winter. Dick Chase, gone to Albany.

I hit my breaking point during the brutal winter of '61. First the Studebaker cracked its frozen engine block on a night when the temperature hit twenty-two below.

Twenty-two below — what am I doing here?

A few nights later I was with some friends, near the end of a slow Monday night ramble, when we finished our last beers and decided to visit Silky Sullivan, whom we hadn't seen all day.

We stood at the door of Silky's apartment, knocked, knocked again. Nobody answered. We opened the door and found the apartment near empty.

And scrawled in lipstick on a mirror:

"Gone to Mexico"

Silky, gone. Books and records gone too, so we knew it was for real.

Some of the others went home. But I went to Jerry Monser's bar. I sat there staring at my beer, on the slump-shouldered side of midnight.

I pounded my fist on the bar, cussed and shouted, "How the hell do I get out of this town?"

And a calm voice said, "First, you take Route Seven."

It was Howie Clark.

Howie had a certain rep. A smooth talker, an operator. But the stories about Howie always had an undercurrent of humor, and he was a welcome fixture on the local bar scene.

Now here he was, reaching for another draft. He raised the mug in a toast, his eyes flickering with a look that said something about trust, and mischief.

"That's the way I've always gone, Howie said. "You take Seven, south. And get warm."

I slid over next to his barstool.

"But how?"

"You just go."

I said, "Right now?"

"Soon as I drink this beer."

He drained it, chin high, and we swung off the barstools and walked out the door. Hitchhiking. Route Seven. Headed south.

*   *   *

That first time, I stayed gone for about three months. Howie and I thumbed our way down to Fort Lauderdale. We crashed at the apartment where Steve Crounse, one of my Oneonta buddies, was living above a restaurant where he worked. Howie and I slept on the floor on a mattress that we wedged into an oversize closet in the mornings.

We later found a house to rent, and it became the party house where visitors chipped in for food and rent.

For a while I parked cars at a hotel. I worked at a Burger King for about two days. But mostly I hung out on the beach with my ukulele, singing, playing popular songs. My memories of those days are of salt spray, sand, sunshine and Coppertone on girl flesh.

This was the beginning of what became the legendary spring break tradition in Fort Lauderdale, and the city was looking for a way to organize the hordes of kids who had nothing better to do than drink, throw up, and get into trouble. I was hired at two dollars a day to play limbos on a stage at the beach. My first professional gig. I was getting paid to do what I would've done for free, and having fun.

I've been operating pretty much the same way ever since.

I had my twentieth birthday, my first away from home, down in Fort Lauderdale. The running house party continued at our place. Howie got the bright idea that girls on vacation could stay there and chip in their money instead of paying rent to a hotel. The only problem was that women iron clothes.

One night, I got fall-down drunk on vodka, stumbled across the ironing board, and smashed my face into the stove. I lay on the floor with my fine Crosby nose pushed to one side, bleeding and swelling.

The house party moved to the hospital for a couple of days where Howie and the gang smuggled in beers and I sang to the nurses with my ukulele. Within days, I was back on the beach, healing in the sun.

Before long, though, spring break ended, and so did the party. Howie headed back to Oneonta. My commitment to the National Guard was on my mind, and I needed a real job so that I could repay my dad for the hospital bills. When Steve Crounse decided to drive back home, I joined him in his overloaded sports car for the long trip back up the East Coast.

I always had a taste for beaches. That's me with the ukulele at one of the first spring breaks in Fort Lauderdale . . . I look like I'm getting away with something, don't I?

We arrived in Oneonta on Easter weekend. As we drove into town I told myself that this return was only temporary.

I knew now that I could get away and make it stick. I didn't mind hitchhiking in the rain. I didn't mind going without a few comforts as long as I was on an adventure. I had no fear of doing it again. In fact, I was willing to live the rest of my life just the way I had lived the past three months. I knew I could do it.

I started tending bar at Jerry's. Danny Brown was back, so we got an apartment again. I had an old leather satchel from Uncle Charlie Galvin, filled it with clothes, and kept it for the next time I left town. The Guard still wouldn't let me transfer until I had a job and an address in the city where I would be moving, but I figured that I could work out these details.

It didn't happen, though. Weeks became months, and I could feel the town closing in around me, pulling me into a life that I didn't want.

The stuck-in-Oneonta blues, again.

Seemed like everybody around me was planning my life for me. Everybody but

"On the road with guitar"

me knew what I should be doing. I felt their expectations. Grow up. Settle down. Face reality. Show some backbone.

I didn't know what I wanted. But I knew it wasn't the life that everyone else wanted for me. I needed a chance, and if I stayed any longer I would never get it.

But that's how it happens. You stay to pay off a debt, then you need a new suit. You get a loan and a new stereo and you're dating this pretty, nice girl. Next thing you know, she's pregnant, and you're getting a bigger apartment. You're married and in debt and wondering what happened to your big adventure. After you retire, you buy a motor home and go looking for that adventure. But the road doesn't mean the same to a seventy-year-old as it does when you're twenty.

One afternoon, as I sat alone in the apartment, I took out the satchel, sat in a chair, and I fell into a deep funk. I knew that I had to get out now if I was going to find what I was looking for in life.

But this time, I would be going AWOL from the Guard, and that meant I would have to cut all ties to Oneonta. I was going to be a fugitive. It would be years — if ever — before I saw the people who meant most to me.

I couldn't even say goodbye. If I told my family what I was planning, they would do everything to stop me.

I had to go. Now.

I picked up the satchel, tossed it out the door into the snow and stared at it there on the ground for the longest time. Then I stepped out the door and picked it up. Numbly, I walked down West End Avenue. Toward Route Seven south. I was trembling as I stuck my thumb out. Right away a car picked me up, took me ten or twelve miles south of town.

There I met Ralph Goodrich, the brother of a guy I had worked with on the beer trucks. He picked me up and listened to my tale as we rode along. When he dropped me off, he handed me twenty dollars and wished me luck.

"Do what you think you have to do, son."

As I stood beside the highway, I promised myself that I would never again let myself feel trapped this way.

I threw away all my identification except for the Jerry Ferris draft card. Ron Crosby no longer existed. It was Jerry Ferris who climbed into the next car headed down the highway.

This was not a road trip. This was the road.

Chapter 2

**Finding laughter and music . . . My portable occupation . . .
Looking down-and-out . . . Go somewhere before you can be
missed . . . New Orleans and Jerry Jeff Walker . . .**

Me and the highway. Thumb out. Trying to land somewhere, sink my teeth into life and take the big bite.

At the cloverleafs, where cars slow and might stop. Under bridges in the rain. Leather satchel and a bass ukulele. Headed south.

I was hiding from no one. Bold-hearted, alive and free. Jerry Ferris, bartender. First name with strangers.

"Jerry." I began to get used to it.

My first stop was Tampa, but the Gulf Coast was still, grey and joyless. I knew there had to be laughter and music out there somewhere, and I caught a ride to New Orleans. Land of Mardi Gras, I'd heard. Whatever that was. Rode the coastal highway, past the gnarled, hurricane-battered oaks, through the pine and scrub.

Driving into Louisiana, along Lake Ponchartrain, I smelled a new air and entered the special magical land of New Orleans. Bought the *Times-Picayune*, February 12, 1963, for the want ads, threw the rest away.

Bartender wanted. Bridge Circle Inn.

Towering over the delta vista, the mammoth Huey P. Long Bridge rises high above the Mississippi River and its lazy flotilla of ships and barges. New Orleans on one side of the river, Bridge City on the other. There, beside the hissing traffic circle, was the Bridge Circle Inn. Faded green highway signs pointed Highway 90 toward Boutte, Houma, and lush swamps, live oaks, Spanish moss and people of character.

I poured the drinks, wiped the bar and listened to the gentle warble of the New Orleans accent. Brown-skinned Cajuns, flush-faced shipyard workers pausing in the doorway before they ambled inside to welcoming shouts from the darkened bar, the joy song of laborers at the end of their work day.

I was bathed with their calm gentle speech, a surprising blend of many tongues. The language of some strange province just outside France or Brooklyn, stroking the morning slowly awake. Mostly kind voices, yapping words, "y'ats" and "dats" and "it doan mattah, Neese."

N'awlins, joyous New Orleans, royal, poor by some unspoken fate, South America washed ashore on the Gulf Coast.

My first place to crash there was a tin-roof shack by the warehouses. Moved in with an old guy who gave me a little cot for fifty cents a day. The two of us lived on flapjacks.

"Flour and water. Just spoon it up," he'd grin through thin gums. He thought sizzling grease was the greatest secret. An old nameless guy and a scrawny wanderer with a new name. He was teaching the kid how to survive.

New city, new people, a new Jerry Ferris. After I had gotten to know the regulars at Bridge Circle Inn, I started walking down to have a few beers at another highway bar. One night, after the jukebox got us all singing, I joined right in with the crowd. Heads turned. The guy who ran the place asked me what I was making over at the Bridge Circle Inn.

"About twenty-five bucks a week. Plus meals."

He said, "Thirty-five bucks."

"Ya got a deal," I grinned.

There's an old road-saying: "Son, what's your portable occupation?" That means a job you can travel with, something to help you get by wherever you land. I wanted to make music, and this new job gave me the chance. It was livelier, more casual and affluent. Not workers in khakis. The rule was that I would work the bar, with my ukulele under the counter. Some nights, the door would burst open and the owner would stride inside, waking up the barroom.

"*Showtime!*" He'd yell across the room, my cue to get the uke out from under the counter and sing something, usually launching "Up A Lazy River." The bartender would work everybody into a party froth, and once we had a pretty good buzz goin', it was "Let's hit the Quarter!"

The French Quarter. I was chauffeur for these excursions. The first time, I had no idea what the Quarter was or what it meant. Behind the wheel of the bar owner's car, I saw destiny. Colorful lights and neon.

Raspy-throated barkers luring sailors and tourists inside to see fat-roll strippers and broad-shouldered transvestites take off their clothes in clubs bathed in dim light. Skinny old black men tap dancing for change outside. Street singers on the corners, voices and guitars and tambourines chattering for some handout money.

The pace was relaxed. The street, vibrant. People laughing, drinking, eating. Music everywhere.

I knew that this was where I needed to be. With about forty dollars in my pocket, I left Bridge City with a one-way ride over the Mississippi River into the Quarter.

One of the first people I ran into was a street singer, Dick Westwell. Older than me, he was about twenty-five. A serious student of the blues. He was playing for pocket change there on the street corners. Dick spent his days picking guitar and hanging out with black street musicians, modeling his music on the sounds of Lightnin' Hopkins, Sonny Terry, Brownie McGhee.

I watched Dick work on 'em but I wasn't much interested in the music. If I liked any blues, it was country blues, like Jimmie Rodgers. I just felt that the real black blues was played better by black people. White kids absorbed it, but they never played it smoothly.

On the streets, I kept playing party stuff. Just good enough for everyone to sing along with me. I mostly made pocket change. Nickels and dimes. Street corners, playing "Scotch and Soda" and other popular tunes which would make people stop to listen.

A Tulane grad school couple into folk music, Harriet and Marty Ottenheimer, ran into me in a club one night. We talked about music and they let me crash on their couch in the early mornings. And they told me right away that I needed to get rid of that ukulele.

"Your voice needs a guitar," Harriet said.

Well then, guitar it was. Nylon-string Mexican job. At first I just played the bottom four strings like a big uke.

Westwell and I got a room in a cheap hotel on Bourbon Street behind Dixieland Hall. One room, two beds, two bucks. Just our price. We could each make a buck in change on the streets and earn a place to stay for the night. The itinerant strippers stayed there while they put together tips for traveling money, as did a few drifting short-order cooks.

"Where you headed? You comin' or goin'?"

"I'm stayin' a spell."

If you came through with a guitar on your back, you were obviously drifting around. And if you were not just one of the deadbeats who sat and stared at the floor, somebody would help you out.

"Hey, I'm trying to get a job here. You know, stop movin' and rest awhile."

A bartender helped us, telling Westwell and me that we looked too preppy, like college kids in from LSU, just drunks with guitars. The tourists wanted to see people who were down and out.

So we bought ratty Levis and Salvation Army shirts. Now we looked funkier. Starting to get into show biz.

We'd tell folks, "Putcher money in the hat."

I was beginning to realize that street performing is a kind of barter. The more talent and entertainment you bring to the sidewalk, the greater your value to the people with change in their pockets. Part of it was image. They were looking for color, wanting me to be different from them, so I became more colorful.

I also began to work at improving my picking and playing.

I learned a lot at a flophouse just past Elysian Fields, an old warehouse with a bunch of cots and old Army blankets. No drinking, out by noon the next day, fifty cents. A lot of regulars were the street singers. We congregated there in the early hours of the morning. One of those was Allen Higgins, a finger-picking student of folk music who could really play.

Allen was patient with me and taught me as best he could. I always preferred learning a song from somebody rather than from a book. I couldn't read music anyway, so I'd listen and watch. It also gave me something to do during the day while I waited to start my evening stroll through the Quarter. I would practice something new every day, either a style or a song or both.

I was singing other people's music, but I wanted to write my own. And one day I did. The bartender who told us to go for the grubby look had another bit of advice. He said that we needed a song to let people know what we were all about. Sort of a musical calling card. So I wrote the verses which later became "Gypsy Songman."

Gypsy Songman

I'm Gypsy Songman, yessir, you'd like to hear my song
Pick it for you now, play it all night long
If the blues is what you seek, this song is what you need
Gypsy Songman, passin' by

My whole life is a song and I'll share it with you now
Pickin' and singin', I'll get by somehow,
A dime would help me, please, a smile is all I need,
Gypsy Songman passin' by

Kids come runnin' as I pass by, they all want to see,
Say "Hey, Gypsy Songman, play a song for me,"
Their eyes glued on my strings, dancin' as I sing,
Gypsy Songman passin' by.

I've got a stage on every corner, got a hall on every street,
My hat is my coin box, this song is what you need
It's just a swap in time, this song is for your dime.
Gypsy Songman passin' by.

So as I leave you now, please remember me this time,
I'm the man who sang a song for your nickels and your dimes.
Today you saw me play as I stopped along the way.
Gypsy Songman passin' by.

Every night I'd head for the corners where tourists entered the Quarter off Canal Street. Floating into my new world, playing street corners for the slow street gawkers of 1963. Awash in the street smells of rotting vegetables and shrimp peelings mulching on the fetid curbs. Old streets. A tangle of walking living, stepping over the bricks and the long-buried bones of the wanderers who'd come before.

Soldiers and hookers and slaves. Corner merchants, barmen, Yankee traders and sailors of those southern seas.

After a rainstorm, their spirits soar up with the mists from that wet steaming stone. In the morning come the living, dragging buckets or hoses, washing away the night puke and blood and wino shit.

This was my new home.

It was a time of pocket change. The road does not pay well. Imagine, the first quarter thrown in your hat, on a cold New Orleans streetlight corner. Nervously, they tossed the money down. Some would walk away in a hurry, making sure that their eyes did not meet mine. But others slowed down a bit. A woman might put her hand

on her husband's arm and pause, listening. Street cor- **"Leaning back in chair"**
ner serenade.

Listen to my song. I play for them to this day, those I can't forget and those I never saw, who felt my eyes and felt the words. Hungry for my song, dancing there on the corner, a soft shuffle to my night guitar. I was child to the romance, playing gypsy to the night.

The Quarter, amazingly, remains the same. The strippers, the smells, the wet sidewalks, the gawkers. Best of all, it's still a place where you can come and do what your life asks you to do. Free to be what you want to be at any time you want. The Big Easy. Always open.

After a while, Westwell and I were accepted into the informal brotherhood of New Orleans street entertainers, including black singers and dancers who had made a proud living this way all their lives.

They'd say, "Harmonica's in my pocket. Taps are on my shoes. I got the whole day ahead of me. Yeah. Free. And I ain't pickin' up shit for nobody and movin' it over there. For nobody. Just bein' me."

One of those guys was Vince Monroe, known as Harmonica Slim. Said he'd teach me to play harmonica if I would come by his house. I had to tell him honestly, "Listen, I barely make enough money to pay rent or eat."

He pointed a finger at me and said, "Wait a minute."

Vince crossed the street directly in front of some tourists. He began to tap and play his harp. With one hand free, he stuck out his hat in front of the tourists. Plop went some change into the hat. He tapped slowly backward as they began to walk again. His feet stopped. Then he ambled back across the street to me and handed me about a buck in loose change.

"Be at my house tomorrow morning," he instructed. "'Bout nine o'clock. No excuse."

I was there, and got my first lesson in harp playing.

New Orleans streets would be my home for several years. But the wanderer got inside me every now and then. I'd hitchhike to Shreveport, Longview, or just across big Lake Ponchartrain to Mandeville or Slidell. You've got to go somewhere before you can be missed.

Thumb out, I would stand under freeway overpasses to stay dry from the rain. My guitar was slung across my back so I could swing it around front and play it for a ride.

During these excursions I discovered the Highway Confessional. I'd get picked up, the driver and I would start to talk. I heard amazing things, secrets these guys wouldn't tell their own wives — things I never ran into in any other setting, even as a bartender. But there, in a car with a complete stranger, the driver might open up his entire life to me.

I've always felt that my years in New Orleans were the equivalent of a college education in life and the world. And those highway confessions were a Master's degree in human nature.

*   *   *

Whenever I returned from the road, I went back to playing the streets of the Quarter with Dick Westwell.

My typical day might be getting up, heading for Minty's, getting a po' boy, a cup of potato salad and Pepsi for ninety-five cents. That left a nickel to call Vic Latham, a bartender at the Old Absinthe House. He let me into his apartment as he went off to work. I would shower, listen to his collection of old blues, maybe jot down some lyrics from one of the records, then hit the streets. I might find one of the other street singers in the park and we'd swap a song for the day. Practice in the corner of the park, then take off to make some money in the bars that night.

We worked the street corners. Passed the hat. A few of the bar owners, late in the evening, would invite Westwell and me inside. This way, when bar-hoppers looked inside, they'd see action, something more than just a jukebox.

One bar gave me a late night job. Around eleven o'clock at night, after an evening of roaming the Quarter and street-singing through the early evening, I would walk over to this little bar off Burgundy and play and pass the hat for a few hours. Eventually they put up a sign outside, advertising when I would play.

The poster said, "Jerry Ferris and his Happy Guitar."

Westwell ragged me hard about that: "*Happy Guitar* — what's that?"

At a corner bar near where "Frogman" Henry played, the bartender looked forward to our arrival.

She was a salty old lady who kind of dug that we'd just bounce in, play, and draw a crowd. Folks would see a lot of people laughing at the bar and maybe a few people

Ryder Coffee House in New Orleans, where I plied my trade in the early 1980s. A magical place where blacks and whites could meet as musicians in that segregated era.

25

applauding after a song. The bar had a little sound system, and we'd just hop up to the microphone and play.

She called me and Westwell "white niggers." She'd croak, "You get in here, pass the hat and make twenty bucks. Now I won't see your ass until you run out of money again."

"Oh, no ma'am. We'll be back," the two of us would assure her.

She'd ruffle our hair and smile, "You guys come back tomorrow night."

"Yes ma'am," we'd say, headed out the door. "We'll be back mañana."

But to a street rounder, mañana meant "possibly never." Maybe tomorrow, maybe mañana.

Twenty dollars in tips would buy several gallon-jugs of cheap wine and maybe a muffuletta from Central Grocery on Decatur. Yeah, those great sandwiches. I'd get one of the big ones, eat part of it, wrap the rest in its paper, and stuff it in a hole in a brick wall or something. Later, after playing the streets, I'd swing by and pick it up for a late meal.

A special treat might be a visit to a couple of coffeehouses, the Ryder and the Quorum, which were helping to shape the French Quarter.

In 1962, a couple of writers, Jack Frazier and Brian Callahan, had rented a shabby two-story wooden building at 910 Rampart Street and turned it into a gathering place that they called the Ryder Coffee House. Less than twenty feet wide, but deep and tall in the New Orleans shotgun style. They sold coffee. No beer, no wine, no whiskey. Maybe cook a stew or make sandwiches. Old sofas, a few chairs, an old coffin for a table.

It was a place for folks to just stand up and sing, pass the hat. Read poetry. Play checkers. Talk about ideas — great ideas and crazy ones.

A big night might draw from ten to twenty people. Hard to call them customers. Mainly they were folks from the neighborhood.

The Ryder was a natural meeting place for musicians, both black and white, to gather, talk, pick and sing. An interesting phenomenon for segregated Louisiana. But in this setting, mixing was just natural. We weren't black or white, we were musicians. We wanted to share songs, and that's hard to do when you've got a wall dividing you.

The Ryder thrived for about a year and closed, followed almost immediately by the opening of the Quorum at 611 Esplanade, that beautiful boulevard smothered in live oaks on the edge of the Quarter. Again, a vigorous mix of intellectuals, college students, street musicians, neighborhood walk-bys.

As they had at the Ryder, blacks and whites mixed freely. We were already integrated as friends, natural friends, unconcerned with the politics of race. We were street musicians, sharing slugs of whiskey on the street, sharing our homes, our music, our lives.

In July of '64, New Orleans police surrounded the Quorum and arrested seventy-three people, many of whom I knew and several of whom would later become very important in my life.

The next day, one of the New Orleans newspapers quoted a police sergeant accusing the Quorum of being the scene of "Communist propaganda, homosexual parties and integration agitation."

Another paper reported, "During the investigation that preceded the raid, two undercover agents stood up and recited extemporaneous poems of 30 minutes each, which, according to the agents, were well received."

Yep, that was the Quorum, all right.

And that was how I lived in those days. Music and the streets and special people and New Orleans magic. To this day, there's a big gap in my knowledge of American pop culture from that period, because throughout those years I never watched TV, never went to a movie. But I didn't miss it. I was too busy living life.

*   *   *

I skipped the bust at the Quorum for the best of reasons. I was on the road, on a long trip that eventually changed my music and my life.

Road adventures were a big part of the existence of the street people I knew, the musicians, writers and painters. The road was the foundation of our charter, and for musicians, it meant the chance to be exposed to different kinds of music.

When the weather got warm, everybody moved. "Goin' where the weather suits my clothes," was a true line from one of the songs. New Orleans was our base, but we were really gypsies, constantly coming and going.

"Westwell's headed to Memphis."

"Allen's gone to Frisco. But Marc's back from New York."

"A new blues singer from Chicago just hit town. He's at the coffeehouse tonight."

That spring, I decided to head east. I remembered Allen Higgins had said that he lived in Richmond, Virginia. He had given me his mom's address and had told me that he planned to be there. I thought I would head that way.

When I hit Richmond I found out Allen was out on the road somewhere. I just drifted toward Virginia Beach. Warm water and sand. I got a job singing in a beachside amusement park during the afternoon. Outside the door was an amusement park where a diver jumped off a 100-foot platform into a barrel of water. My singing was supposed to drag in some of the folks who had gathered to watch the dive.

Waiting to go on at the Main Point in Bryn Mawr, Pennsylvania, in 1969 . . . This might be the last time I wore a tie onstage.

One afternoon I was playing way down at the end of the bar for maybe three people who weren't even looking at me. In walked this tall guy with a beard, a pillowcase thrown over one shoulder, a beat-up guitar in the other hand. He strode the length of the place, sizing up the joint. Stopped right in front of me while I was singing.

"What the hell are you doing in here?" he said to me.

I kept pickin', but moved my head off microphone.

"I was just thinking that myself."

"Let's get out of this dump," he declared.

"Yeah," I decided. "Just thinking that myself."

I swung my guitar behind my back, walked over to the bartender and asked for the day's pay.

"Stoney" was how my bearded, grinning new acquaintance introduced himself.

We found a neighborhood bar and proceeded to swap road stories. After a few hours, a couple of guys in the place eased over and asked about the guitars. We broke them out and proceeded to sing for free drinks, even some loose change. That night one of the locals offered us a place to stay, but we just took a ride from him to the edge of town. There was a great night coming, bringing a beautiful morning, and we wanted to be on the road when it arrived.

Stoney and I spent three or four days winding our way through the mountains of West Virginia, then into Ohio. We told one long tale after another, trying to outdo each other.

Swapped a lot of music. One of us would stick his thumb out, the other would pick. We were working our way toward Ohio, because Stoney had a brother near Cincinnati he wanted to visit.

Stoney

I first ran into Stoney, in some bar downtown.
It was Richmond, Virginia then, bummin' around
Suitcase to suitcase, we started in talkin',
Findin' 'bout the things we shared, and all the miles we'd been.

Now in this gray pillowcase were some books by Durrell,
And an old concertina, beat up and played like hell.
Until you got him singing old gospel songs,
He drank all night for nothing and told stories till dawn.

He said, "Come on, grab your bag, boy, sun's up, now it's time to go.
You know morning's just about the right time for starting down a road.
Feeling a new day start 'stead of just rushing on by.
Like I'm some Mr. Independence taking my own sweet time."
So we walked on out that highway, clear blue sky,
Listening to the tales he told, drinking warm red wine,
The time he made sixes, that chick he done wrong,
All the things he dreamed about while we walked along.

The old Stoney had a magic made him hard to forget,
Like that night we flew down the highway, that pickup truck nearly wrecked,
With a crazy woman driving, she's drunk and carrying on,
Till Stoney finally calmed her with a gospel song.

Yeah, we split the road at Norwood, he just shook my hand,

He said, *"I'll see you someplace,"* but he never has.
Yeah, we were that free then, walking down the road,
Never really caring where the highway goes.

Now maybe Stoney was a liar, yeah, there's no doubt about it,
For just the way he told, and why you'd never want to doubt him,
'Cause he kept you going when the road got tough,
And he brought you through all the lean times by making it up.

"Standing at crossroads"

Guess the last ride we took was the capper to the whole trip. A drunk hillbilly woman picked us up in an old Buick.

It was foggy as hell and she was driving with a can of beer on the dash. Every corner we'd go around, she'd grab that beer as it slid across the dash, the full length of the windshield. One hand on the wheel, one catching the beer.

"Stoney," I suggested, eyes wide, "why don't we think about playin' a little something here."

He broke into "Just A Closer Walk With Thee," and she slowed down to sing along. He stopped, she speeded up. We wanted the ride, but we didn't want to die for it. That night, I discovered that Stoney knew a shitload of gospel music.

As we finally climbed out of the car near Cincinnati, Stoney said "My brother is a folkologist, and his field of expertise is gospel music. Field recorder, all that stuff. I've heard hours and hours of that music."

Good thing, too. Probably saved our asses that night.

We shook hands, and he went off into Cincy. I headed on to Chicago where I wanted to check out the folk scene. Maybe some of my New Orleans road brothers would be driftin' that way too. But Chicago turned out to be too slick for my taste, the music citified and businesslike.

Truth was, I wasn't good enough yet either.

I hung around awhile, though, and eventually met a young singer from Columbus, Ohio, Eddie Watson. He mentioned a nice scene in his hometown. Coffeehouses, lots of bluegrass and students. He gave me the names of a couple of places. So I drifted off in that direction. Anywhere but the big windy city.

I spent the rest of the summer in Columbus, Ohio. I hadn't planned to stay that long, but through a series of coffeehouse acquaintances I met Joan and Miles Gibbons.

Miles taught art at Ohio State and played a mean bluegrass guitar. Joan was deeply involved in the music scene in Columbus. They were the kind of people I had come to appreciate in New Orleans — bright, eclectic, free-thinking. Visitors were always welcome at their house, and most of them showed up to make music. I spent so much time there that I finally just moved in with them.

There was always somebody picking in that house, and I tried to absorb it all. It was full-time immersion in music, me and my guitar, day and night.

I decided to learn or write a new song every day. Woody Guthrie, Jimmie Rodgers, Ramblin' Jack Elliott, Bob Dylan, Brownie McGhee, Doc Watson and any songs being sung by the people coming through the Gibbons house. I was doing what all musicians have done forever, borrowing a little of this, plugging in a little of that and, bam, a new song.

I had come north with a small Martin Guitar 00018 some nice divorcee had laid on me after I'd laid on her nicely. A sweet guitar, but I really wanted a big old Gibson. That summer I spotted one over in a music store in Columbus. It was a Roy Smeck Stage Deluxe. Part Dobro, part flattop.

I traded in the old Martin for the Roy Smeck. The owner-repairman said the Martin was worth more than the Smeck, so he evened things out by shaving down the neck of the Gibson, putting smaller guitar frets on it.

"Now, that'll play," he assured me. "Play real nice."

It looked more like me, too. Not as fancy as the Martin, but it had a wonderful sound when flat-picked. It never left my side.

The really big event for my music that summer was a concert at Oberlin College with Doc Watson and Ramblin' Jack. Doc blew us all away with his great guitar playing, storytelling and harmonica. I was totally captivated by Ramblin' Jack. The way he just threw off songs. He yodeled, he flat-picked, he rambled on with long-winded stories. I realized that he took his name from his talking, not his traveling.

Those performances changed the direction of my music. This was how I wanted to play and sing. If I could pick like Doc and tell stories like Jack and write songs all my own, that would be my niche.

*   *   *

As the year got into fall and the weather started to get colder, I decided to make tracks south. I headed back to New Orleans.

Hitting the Quarter again felt like coming home. My first night back, I hit one of my favorite spots, the Quorum on Esplanade, scene of the mass bust that summer.

Walked in to find a big, 6-foot-5 guy standing up, reciting some lusty account of angels and sex, a satyr's mischievous leer stretched across his face.

His name was Ben Jennings, and before the night was done, he and his wife, Char, invited me and another musician to have dinner the next night at their apartment on Governor Nicholls Street.

I was the only one who showed for dinner, and Ben and I spent a lot of time that night talking and connecting.

Ben was in his mid-twenties. He had confidence from a tour in the Marines but none of the hard edges. Booming, joyous laughter filled any room where Ben presided. Always talking, always telling stories. Loud, bawdy stories, wine glass swirling in the air for punctuation. Stories of new love or old lovers, endlessly streaming.

"Let's walk the streets, give tips to the bums," he'd sparkle. "And oh, let's keep talking as we walk."

"Yes!" with booming enthusiasm was Ben's favorite roar.

Right away, Ben and I became extremely good friends. He and Char didn't have much, but none of us did. He offered me a mattress in the corner of his apartment.

Ben looked down at the mattress and asked, "This gonna be good enough?"

"Well," I told him, "when you're on the couch circuit, you don't thump melons."

People had a way of attaching themselves to Ben, and he never resisted. I guess he felt he was big and strong enough to carry us all. Deckey Moat, a high school dropout, had moved in as permanent baby sitter for Ben and Char's two kids. And she was looking after Ben in many interesting ways. Ben, in true character, had also started an affair with a Tulane student, Linda Burris.

Giving the body what it needs is a simple job. Give the body what it wants and you've got a never-ending task. Late at night, the apartment whispered with scurrying feet, often size 13, moving from room to room.

Even the sexual revolution had its limits, though. When Char caught little Deckey wearing Char's underwear, the sharing ceased. Curses exploded in the apartment. Char reached to hurl a bottle of Jack Daniel's at Ben, but I grabbed the bottle first and dashed out the door with it. Ben and I watched from the street as a torrent of his clothing, books and drawings came flying out the door.

The door closed and locked. My Roy Smeck was still inside. Ben, Linda Burris and I loaded scattered items into a car and drove off, stunned and chuckling.

Well, a good guitar is hard to replace. I went back later that evening to retrieve the Smeck and spent the night in Char's bed.

One good thing about being a street rambler, you don't have to make excuses about where you spend the night. Couple of nights later, I ran into Ben and Linda at La Casa down on Decatur. I had the guitar slung across my shoulder.

"Hey," they said. "You got it back!"

I mumbled something. "Yeah. Needed it."

Ben and Linda doubled over. "She got you! Ha! She got you with that guitar."

"Yeah, and I had to convince her that the guitar wasn't the reason I came back."

All this led to Ben getting a new apartment several blocks away. Right above Two Jays Bar, Governor Nicholls at Decatur Street. Up a rickety staircase, into a sweeping series of empty rooms. Ben was in love again, with Linda Burris. And as in all of his pads, as with his varied romances, Ben shared. We crashed into the place, nothing more than a bed and an old thin mattress by the window.

As usual, I worked the Quarter at night, coaxing nickels and dimes. Sometime before dawn, I would return from the streets, prop my guitar in the brick corner by the cracked plaster, lay off my boots and stand them up beside the guitar, and fall onto the mattress across the room from Ben and Linda.

Above his bed, on the wall, Ben had drawn a magnificent angel, a grand swooping beautiful lady angel. Swirling dark hair blossoming, her arm reaching down the wall from the heavens, one finger outstretched to lightly bless Ben's bed with a touch.

Ben had a job at a warehouse. He would wake up about six, slowly rising for work. I always woke up when he did, gave a first yawn and then reached for my guitar. I'd strum and sing as I lay on the mattress, trying out new songs for Ben while Linda acted like she wasn't playing with his privates beneath the sheets, which she always was.

Ben would work until late afternoon. I made a point to have a jug of red paisano wine waiting for him when he returned. My little tribute, bought with the change I had pulled in the night before. I admired the way Ben held down that job, day after day, to pay the rent and buy the groceries.

It was a joyous, free time in our lives. A time of love and constant adventure and curiosity about what awaited us around the corner.

Magical.

*   *   *

Out on the sidewalk in front of Ben's apartment sat a shoeshine stand that was a neighborhood gathering place for street singers and blues musicians. At any time in the evening you might hear a singer or two, dancers, banjo, harmonica, people just drifting by and stopping to create some impromptu beauty. Hands patting time, slapping thighs.

In New Orleans I came alive among those black pickers and singers. Their music wasn't really my music, but I loved the joy and feeling and spontaneity that they brought to their playing.

"Ben's magnificent angel"   One of the first black street singers who caught my attention was Babe Stovall. His first steady work in New Orleans was doing carpentry for Sam Jaffe, who ran Preservation Hall. Sam had a music store of old blues records and an art gallery. On weekends Babe would pick by the gallery front door. Babe was good. He played a wooden Dobro with a metal resonator, using a finger-picking style of country blues and gospel.

Babe had grown up around Tylertown, Mississippi, picking tung nuts, working in the groves. He claimed he'd sold a pig to buy his first guitar. He had taught himself to play by watching and listening to the music of Tommy Johnson.

Soon he was playing parties and beer joints around Tylertown, then living for a spell in Franklinton, Louisiana. Like many before him, Babe was eventually drawn to New Orleans. He had been playing at the Quorum on the night of the summer police raid.

One day Ben and I ran across Babe walkin' the streets. He wasn't going anywhere in particular, so we dragged him into a courtyard bar for a beer. Soon Babe and I were picking. At first, we just played for each other. Kind of checking out each other's style.

After a while, Babe told us he played regularly at Snyder's Bar down on Decatur Street.

He said, "Now, 'f you come by, bring a jug witcha. We'll pick some."

Next evening, we hooked up with him at Snyder's and spent the rest of the night picking by the levee. We quit about daylight, with Babe on the guitar, me playing harp and Ben playing the bass parts on the empty bottle of Ten High whiskey, Babe's brand.

Babe lifted the dregs of the whiskey in a paper cup, and proclaimed to the night sky:

"Here's to the duck that swum a lake
and never lost a feather

may this time another year
we all be together."

I had found a new friend.

*   *   *

In one of those Quarter bars, on one of those nights late in 1964, Fate walked in for a drink. I was between sets when I glanced around the room and spotted a familiar face in one of the booths.

"That's Jack Baker."

Jack Baker, from Oneonta, New York. Jack Baker, one of Silky Sullivan's roommates. Jack Baker, the company clerk from my hometown National Guard unit where I'd been AWOL for many months.

"Shit. They've come to get me."

With a saunter and maybe a nervous swagger, I strolled over to his booth and plopped down next to him.

"I surrender."

"Oh my God." Baker recoiled, swearing through a mouthful of beer.

"Did they send you down here to arrest me?"

"Fuck no," Baker snorted. "I'm the last guy they'd send for anybody. I'm out of the Guard. Signed on with the Navy again. I'm in port here. Just having a beer."

We told lies for a few minutes. Baker stared at the foam at the bottom of his glass. He was contemplating confession.

He said, "I don't think they even know you're gone."

I stared at him. He looked me deadpan in the eyes, then began to laugh through his nose, a staccato of tiny explosions. Faint wisps of beer misted from his nostrils.

"The last time you split," he said, "I just left your name on the records. You're still probably makin' roll call."

My eyes began to widen. My back straightened.

"What you oughta do," Baker whispered, "is go back and get it all cleared up for good. If they've screwed up your records, they're likely to make a deal with you. And your folks need to hear from you, too."

That advice hit me hard. I knew that my sudden departure must've hurt my family. Mel, Alma, and Grandma Jessie hadn't heard from me at all. I'd left them no clue where I was or even whether I was still alive. My sadness about that was always in the back of my mind.

I also knew that I wanted to travel outside the U.S. one of these days — Mexico, Puerto Rico, Rio de Janeiro — but Jerry Ferris could never get a passport.

This was a chance to set some of that straight.

I hitchhiked back to Oneonta. Went to see my folks first. They saw me walking up the road, a fuller, taller man now. Beat-up hat, shirttail out, pants tucked into cowboy boots.

I looked like a road person, which I was.

It was a tense, bittersweet day. We talked around much of the heartache, set-

Babe took me under his wing and showed me the street-singing ropes in New Orleans years ago. A great gentleman and musician. He used to say, "A lean dog can run a long race."

tling instead for just having the family together again. My kid sister, Cheryl, was virtually seeing me for the first time. She had been born to my parents as a surprise child when I was in my mid-teens. Although I would often baby-sit with her when she was an infant, we had never really known each other. Now she was a little grade-school kid peering at her grown older brother. Shyly peeking out of her bedroom. Glancing up at me as she walked by.

The next afternoon, I was walking into the Oneonta National Guard armory, that temple of ghost shouts of basketball games and military drills. I had combed my hair and put on some old clothes from high school days that my folks still had.

I was ready for the worst. I knew that desertion was a jailing offense.

The company commander held my personnel folder in front of him. Military records of PFC Ronald C. Crosby. He was new, and he'd been busy.

"Since I got in here," he said, "I've been cleaning up a lot of old business.

We see you've had, well, pretty much a hit-and-miss deal with the U.S. military."

"Yeah." I offered, saying no more, waiting. Thinking that my true service record for those two missing years would show a Purple Heart for a broken nose at spring break, and a long tour of duty in the French Quarter.

He fingered the two-page document in front of him, names and transfers and records of assignment. One line said it all:

**CROSBY, RONALD C 22009819 PFC E3 Co
C 2 ARB 108 Inf eff 12 Mar 63 ETS 24 Jul 63**

That garble apparently meant that on March 12, 1963, the New York National Guard had given up on missing Ron Crosby, yet had awarded me time of service until July 24, three years after I'd been sworn in.

"We saw that you'd been on the books long after you were gone," the commander said, closing my file. "Looked bad for our records. So what we did was put you on permanent standby reserve."

The commander looked dead-eyed across the desk. His voice went dry and firm.

"To tell the truth, we didn't expect to see your ass any more."

My voice cracked, "I believe you won't, sir."

"That'll be all, son. You're dismissed."

I walked numbly out of the captain's office and down a flight of stairs. I pulled open the front door and stepped out into the fresh air.

Freedom. Free to go. Free to go anywhere. Free to be anybody I wanted to be.

Down two more flights of steps to the street. During this floating walk down, it dawned on me that Jerry Ferris no longer existed. The man on the run could now walk away. I decided to christen myself with a new name.

The name I chose, almost on the spot, was Jeff Walker.

It was partly as a tribute to Kirby Walker, a colorful black jazz pianist who had befriended me many times by calling me up from the crowd to sing with him.

Partly, because I just liked the name Jeff. Jeff Walker. Just liked the name. I was going to be Jeff Walker. That was it.

Two weeks later, the newborn Jeff Walker was back in New Orleans. I hadn't wasted a whole lot of time getting out of Oneonta. Back into the streets and the bars where I ran into a problem.

I had been in New Orleans long enough by now to make a name for myself, and that name was Jerry Ferris. Even my friends wouldn't let me be Jeff Walker.

Real people don't change their names. Even when I tried to name myself, I couldn't. I was stumped until the solution came to me after several glasses of wine with Ben Jennings and Linda Burris, with both of them insisting that I had to stay Jerry, because that's how everybody knew me.

Fast-forward to a couple of nights later, a bar in the Quarter, red spotlight blasting an empty stool on a tiny stage, beefy bouncer clutching a microphone in his hand.

The bouncer yells into the mike, punching every word.

"Ladies and Gentlemen. Live. In New Awlins, Lews'yana.

"Jerry!

"Jeff!

"Walker!"

Chapter 3

Babe and the National. . . That old, beat-up guitar . . . Lessons from a Thanksgiving day . . . Walking out doesn't mean the end of your existence . . . 'I gotta do this' . . .

New Orleans was not just street entertainers and tourists and atmosphere. It was also a haven for artists, writers, free-thinkers and the generally bent and unconventional. If you lived in the South in the '60s, and you were just a little bit different, New Orleans was where you belonged.

I jumped right into the middle of this culture. The liberated atmosphere. The constant exchange of ideas and questioning of assumptions was unlike anything I had known in Oneonta. I guess hundreds of thousands of young people over the centuries have found the same kind of exhilaration in the openness of New Orleans.

But this was my time. My life.

The best part was Ivan's Wine Discussion Group, Monday night gatherings in a smoky upstairs apartment where a couple of gay poets lived. You'd come in and put into the pot whatever money you could spare, and somebody'd go buy the wine. Usually gallon jugs of Gallo. Pass it around, pouring cheap red into paper cups. We'd drink and talk about art, literature, our sex lives, anything that came to mind in an hours-long open house.

This was heady stuff to a small town lad from upstate New York.

Ben would be there, towering above the clatter, catching me up on things if I arrived late: "Jerry, we've got a full rant going tonight. Tekla's already crying because we're talking about her son in the mental institution. Helen's threatening to leave if I mention Jean Genet one more time. Vernon's raising his hands, moaning, 'Leave. Leave.' It's all primed and delicious!"

People would scream, stomp out, spill wine and cluster-argue. If the discussion was about music, you'd likely have a person on one side talking about opera, a person on another side talking about Leadbelly, and the two of them trying to communicate with you in the middle.

Three of four hours, long enough for several folks to get really drunk. And at the

"With Babe on bench" end, fiery. Two people might wander off to the bathroom to have sex while two others were trying to kill each other, or at least threatening it. Heady stuff indeed.

I'd never been around such people. Until now all the people I had known over thirty were all selling insurance. But here were writers and thinkers and drifters. Painters, poets, madmen. They made their living bartending and at other fringe occupations in the Quarter.

Whenever I returned to the Quarter from hitchhiking around the country, I'd bring back new songs that I had learned or written. The regulars at the Monday night group were a great audience as I tried out new styles and ideas.

This was the new life I had promised myself for all those restless years.

One Monday night after the gathering broke up, I found myself sitting down by the river drinking wine with a raging visionary poet. Page by page he was tossing his writing into the Mississippi. He would read to the night then toss a page. Tenderly beautiful poems, strange haunting babbles and giant epics. He had stayed up many painful mornings scratching these in solitude. And now he was watching a freighter pass under night clouds and throwing all that work into the river.

"None of it's any good," he reasoned without reason.

I was too young to judge, but I thought the act itself was magical and poetic.

Just as I had done with Uncle Charlie Galvin back in Oneonta, I began to gorge on books, minds and conversation.

Ben turned me on to a lot of writing, a lot of Genet. And I was enthralled with Kenneth Patchen's "The Journal of Albion Moonlight," a fevered nightmare of whispers around a campfire. Conversations while slightly euphoric. Illusionary bullshit, disjointed, like notes jotted down in haste and stashed in a backpack by the road.

It's still one of my favorite books. Makes me wish that I'd kept a journal all those years.

I read it with a fresh heart, a new mind. I think that's when you are at your best — your most emotional, most loving — when you look at the world with little-boy eyes.

That was me those days in New Orleans.

*   *   *

Babe Stovall and I had become great friends, sharing music, laughter and pints of whiskey. The two of us were starting to play together at a few of the nicer bars around the Quarter, often at Cosimo's Bar on Burgundy.

Babe and I were constantly searching each other out, playing clubs or park benches, it really didn't matter. He was my good friend. We could talk. Babe had that cheap old guitar, which he could make sing like a second voice. He brought heaven a little closer down, just so heaven could listen.

One Friday night, we were at Ben's. Ben loved to come home from work and find a lot of action in his place, and this was one big-ass party. People were everywhere, Ben holding forth in his favorite corner. Two young black kids in their twenties, down from Southern University, had fallen in with our group.

Babe said, "I sho' could sing better if'n I had a little whiskey on my throat."

These two uptown guys jumped to their feet, "We'll go get it for you." And before Babe finished the next song, they were back.

They passed a brown paper bag around the room, a trail of snorts and pinched eyes following it. When the bottle got to Babe, he took a pull and immediately winced and wrinkled his nose.

"Oooh. Oh, Gawd. What is dis stuff?"

Babe pulled the sack off, revealing a bottle of premium scotch. He pushed the bottle back in the bag and handed it to the young guys who'd gotten it for us.

Babe leaned over to me, saying "Jer'uh, I believes we're gonna need another run to the store."

We took up a collection in my hat, made a run for Ten High, and we were back in business.

That was the night Marc Ryan, a young blues enthusiast from New Jersey, showed up with the National.

Big, heavy, chrome-plated guitar, a Hawaiian sunset engraved on the back. Steel-bodied, bright and shiny and loud.

He had found it used, at a music store. He showed it around, proud.

Eventually it came around to the master. Babe took it for a spin. Real strong for a couple of songs. The National easily matched Babe's powerful voice.

Suddenly Babe stopped. "How much you pay for dis?" he asked, stroking the shiny body.

"Eighty bucks," Marc replied timidly.

Babe thought real hard. The room settled into a moment's quiet.

"Give you eighty-five." Babe said proudly.

We all just roared with laughter. "C'mon Marc! That's a great deal!"

Marc was blushing, but he had his wits about him: "I'll make you a better deal. You teach me to play like you just played, and I'll swap guitars with you flat out."

We all cheered. Babe was grinning like a cat with a mouse. He walked out that night with a new guitar and a new student.

Babe always seemed to have a following of young musicians and would-be's who hung out with him, basking in his genius and hoping to catch a little of the Stovall magic. He was the real thing, and we all knew it. After Babe acquired the National, his acolytes came in handy. It was heavy, like carrying an anvil, and when Babe walked the Quarter, one or another of us would tote it for him.

Which is probably how we came to count the steps up to Bob Fisher's apartment. Bob didn't play, he didn't sing. But Bob was important to Babe and to me and a number of other struggling artists.

Bob was a top-dollar engineer working on a missile project, but his heart was into music, not warheads. He loved our scene and wanted badly to walk away from the world and run away with the rest of us in the great adventure of our lives. We were always welcome at his place, which was on one of the upper floors of an apartment building without an elevator. Late at night, we'd head to Bob's, and Babe would stop us at the bottom of the stairs.

"Jer'uh, I want you to count the steps up to Bob Fisho's. There's eighty-nine of them."

"I know, Babe, we counted 'em last time."

Babe wanted us to know that this climb was going to be the last thing we were going to do that day.

"So don't talk about goin' anywheres else."

Somebody hauled Babe's National. And we counted out loud.

"One, two, three," all voices chanted. Except Babe's. Babe just climbed.

Our days were usually spent in Jackson Square. The park itself surrounds the statue of Andrew Jackson on his mount. We'd sit on the park benches and Babe might play something new, something we'd not heard before. We would all take notice and try to play it ourselves.

Pretty soon we'd be up to speed and a crowd would gather. I'd push my hat out in front of us. The crowd, sitting cross-legged on the grass all around us. The hat filling.

Babe said to me, "Jer'uh. Jer'uh. Think it's time we head for Johnny Matassa's. I'm gettin' thu'sty."

"Babe, we got us a crowd, a big crowd. We oughta milk it for all it's worth."

Babe shifted around on the bench, his shoulders anxious. Reset his hat on his head and stood up. Pulled on his belt, tugging up his pants, and set his jaw.

"Jer'uh. Just 'cause a horse'll go don't mean you gotta ride it to death."

So we headed for Johnny Matassa's with a hatful of money. Matassa's, a throwback bar like I'd never seen before. A corner grocery with a long bar inside. Along one street were two doors, one at each end of the bar. One marked "colored," the other "white only." It was all one building, one bar, but a wall divided everything in half. Same bartender served both sides. If I sat at the bar by the wall that divided "colored" from "white only" I could lean over, look around the wall, and talk to Babe on the other side. We usually drank one cold one there, then got some beer or cold wine from the store and moved on.

The Dream Castle was a little bar across Elysian Fields in the black neighborhood run by a guy named Snyder.

"On park bench"

"Snydo," Babe called him.

We went down there Thursday or Friday nights to play. They'd turn the jukebox off. The place would be packed. No air conditioning, even in the New Orleans summer. There'd be people smokin', sweatin', drinkin'. And we'd set up in the corner to play.

Marc Ryan was with us. We had a jug band and harmonicas. For us to be accepted into that crowd at Snyder's bar meant we must have been playing pretty good music.

Babe had this running feud with "Snydo" over a little bit of everything, especially about getting paid.

One time Babe complained that the room was too hot.

So Snyder got a big kitchen fan, big-ass thing about five feet high, four feet wide, and put it right behind where we sat to play. It roared. Just about blew us off our chairs. We tried a couple of songs.

Babe stopped playing, stood, tugged at his pants for emphasis, and announced to the entire bar, "Either Babe Stovall plays. Or the fan plays. But Babe and the fan do not play together."

A few days later Babe went back into the bar alone, waving a great big hawg-leg pistol, trying to get some money that he believed "Snydo" owed us.

After that, we had to find a new place to play music.

Babe was very patient with his young followers. And he took great pains to play

"The Angel guitar"

his licks for us, though he always left something out just to keep his music special.

One night Babe wanted to try my new Roy Smeck. He took the Gibson and began thumping out "Time Is Winding Up" as loud as I'd ever heard him play, picking it with his big thumb pick. He threw it up behind his head and started dancing around. When he handed it back, after three or four songs, I noticed a gouge on the on the top. He had been playing so hard that he dug a small trench where his pick slapped the wood.

I borrowed a nail clipper and asked Babe to scratch his name by the marks.

A few days later, I asked Ben Jennings to add one of his drawings to the top of the guitar.

I left it with him, and a couple of days later dropped by his place.

"The seduction of the oval!" he thundered as he presented it to me.

He had drawn a lady, an angel. Hair flowed around her face as her arms reached back to caress the sound hole.

"The Angel." I was stunned.

"The Angel," Ben beamed.

That Old Beat-Up Guitar

CHORUS
> Well I found her in a pawn shop
> Somewhere up in Ohio,
> Where I guess some rounder came up short
> And he had to let her go.
> It cost me ninety dollars,
> But it's worth much more by far.
> 'Cause I never had a better friend
> Than that old beat-up guitar.
> It didn't look like too much,
> Just a Roy Smeck Stage Deluxe,
> But a lady never fared as well
> Who traveled through so much.

She traveled with me always
Through the alleys and the bars,
And the songs I sang and friends I knew
were part of that guitar.
Some nights it was my pillow
Restin' underneath the stars,
And day and night I stayed alive
With that old beat-up guitar.

(Repeat Chorus)

She picked up the name of Angel
In an old New Orleans bar
Where a drunken poet drew one
On top of that guitar.
And ol' Babe Stovall marked her
Scratching songs right from his heart
Seems everyone that used her
Scarred the old beat-up guitar

(Repeat Chorus)

A ramblin' man has trouble
Hangin' on to all that he owns
And in the years of travelin'
That guitar fell by the road
Till one night in New Mexico
I wandered into this bar
Where the Angel lay a-smilin'
On that old beat-up guitar.

(Repeat Chorus)

I took her from the wall
And ran my hands across the scars
And I played again the old songs
That were written on that guitar.
An' friends I'd loved and lost
Too many nights inside of a bar
Come back so clearly
Singing with that old beat-up guitar.

(Repeat Chorus)

Now she travels with me always
Through the alleys and the bars
And the songs I sing and friends I know
Are part of that guitar
And some nights it is my pillow
Restin' underneath the stars
And day and night I stay alive
With that old beat-up guitar.

(Repeat Chorus)

*   *   *

By the fall of 1964, Babe and I had begun to play every Thursday night at Cosimo's on Burgundy. Good money, sometimes almost $100 apiece in tips. And Thanksgiving Thursday would be a big night for us.

Ben Jennings had heard about a Thanksgiving dinner being organized by Babe's nephew and his nephew's wife. They were poor, but had warmly invited many folks from their neighborhood over to their place to eat. They told us to come over, too. We figured we couldn't come unless we contributed our share and more. Ben threw in what was left of his paycheck, but we still needed more food for the feast.

So we organized the Great Winn-Dixie Thanksgiving Shoplifting Adventure.

We all had assignments. A shopping list for young rounders, felonious behavior familiar to college students and the young poor. Barbara headed for the butter. I slipped down one aisle. And looming in the doorway, complete with trench coat of many pockets, was Fagin himself, Ben Jennings.

Back at the apartment, we unloaded our plunder while Ben headed down Decatur Street to a live poultry market — not an unusual sight in the Quarter at that time. Reasonable rascals that we were, we had figured that stealing a turkey was out of the question.

We trundled over to Babe's nephew's house with our bounty and found the cooking in progress, many of the neighbors already there. Babe was holding court. The women and a bunch of running, chasing children were in the kitchen. But when we presented the twenty-five pounds of potatoes we'd brought, a few faces fell and the peeling quickly became tedious and a drag.

I went over to Babe. "Hey, let's have some fun doing this. Git your guitar out."

Babe and I started playing and made up a song, more like a chant. A beat about cooking, strumming and singing it to music. The tiny kitchen with its one sad solid table turned into a celebration as the cooks called back the refrain.

> *Peel those potatoes*
> > *Peel those potatoes*
> *Peel those potatoes*
> > *Peel those potatoes*

And we made up a little blues song right there, just me and Babe and our guitars. Ben wailing harmonica over a sack of potatoes. All of a sudden, the women had finished peeling, and Babe and I were only half done with our song.

As the feast began to cook, Babe's nephew and friends eased into a jam session. The whole neighborhood was there, making some of the best music I had ever heard. Totally improvisational. Everybody was playing pots and pans and thinking up verses. It was a great moment. We were celebrating Thanksgiving, celebrating friends and music.

It was the most wonderful Thanksgiving I could imagine. And when it began drawing dark, it was time for Babe and me to head to Cosimo's for our gig. The rest of them wanted to keep the party going, so the whole bunch of us descended en masse on Cosimo's. Thanksgiving Day 1964, in the segregated South.

We got to Cosimo's, and I went to the owner and told him about our situation: "We've spent the whole day together and it would be nice if Babe's family could sit over by the stage with us and watch our show."

He said, "No niggers in my joint."

"Well, they'll be kind of like with the band, in our area," I reasoned.

"No way," he pronounced. "Just you and Babe, that's it."

I walked sheepishly to Babe, waiting by the door.

"Babe, they're not gonna let your family in. What you want to do?"

Babe puffed up his chest, hiked up his pants with his thumbs. "Jer'uh. I makes money. Money don't make me."

I Makes Money (Money Don't Make Me)

CHORUS:
> *I makes money, money don't make me*
> *That's the way I am and it's plain to see.*

Get right for yourself, they can't put you on a shelf.
Live and let live, you know it's plain enough.
There ain't a dollar in the world can make me change my stuff.

If you find yourself waiting and you know you're hesitating, get your butt off the ground.
It ain't money or your honey, and you know it's kind of funny when it's all boiled down.

If you want to be the man, and you know you certainly can, then do it, do it, do it, do it, do it.
Clothes don't make the man, money won't make you stand any truer than you're doin'.

I met lots of men who told me when they finally make their first million
They're gonna live like kings, gonna try everything.
They're gonna flatter pretty women, why not get to it
Instead of waiting all your life, 'cause life is only doing what you think is worth pursuing, instead of waiting all the time.

CHORUS

So you'll never find the endin' of sitting and pretending.
You're gonna do it sometime, you keep knocking on wood,
Doing exactly what you should, trying to save enough dimes.
Build 'em up higher, so you can retire
To your castle in the blue, but you find it's all behind and it's probably slipped your mind, and you're too pooped to toot.

CHORUS

And with that we walked away, and walked out on the best gig we had.

With about thirty people in tow, we headed down the street to a loft where we'd heard that a big party would be going. And man, was it going.

When we got there, they said, "You and Babe set up there in the corner."

Me, Babe, Babe's family, sittin' cross-legged on the floor.

"Can we pass the hat, too?" we hollered over the party noise.

"Yeah. Hell, yeah."

We put the hat on the floor. Made almost as much money as we would have made at Cosimo's.

We had a great time, making the best of the situation. We just didn't have a job for next Thursday. But if you can't do what you want as a street singer, when *will* you do it?

It was not the first time, nor the last, that I walked away from steady money. I have learned that walking out on a situation you don't like doesn't mean the end of your existence.

* * *

That fall in New Orleans, I felt for the first time that I was all together. I had a solid repertoire of songs, some bluegrass, some country, folk songs and things of my own. I was playing the Angel with a harmonica on a neck rack. I moved about the Quarter like I owned the place. I knew bartenders and club owners. I could spot two or three couples moving through the Quarter, step into their path, and present myself as a true street character.

"Drop the money right into the sound hole, doesn't hurt a bit. Dollar bills are softer."

I wouldn't stop to pass the hat because they got away. They'd plop the money right into the Angel. I had regular bars to pop into early in the evening and start things off. People would look in and be drawn in for a beer or two. That would be between eight and nine o'clock. Then I'd go meet Babe at one of our regular stops.

I was steadier in another way, too. A few months earlier I had moved into an apartment with Barbara Lyons, a young woman who had quit her job as a secretary in New York and come to New Orleans for some of the same reasons most everybody else does, to just let loose and roll with life. She was a good-looking brunette, totally independent, with a free-wheeling spirit.

Barbara and I shared a powerful attraction, and we spent every day together, cartwheeling through life. We were both free to experience and experiment, but we gravitated toward each other more than just a little. The word was hard to say in those days, but yeah, it was becoming love.

Barbara was stability amid years of rambling. I liked the feeling of a warm woman in a warm room.

In all, it was probably as close as a street singer can come to a settled life and a steady livelihood. This is probably part of the reason I started to get restless.

After barely escaping Oneonta, I was wary of getting involved with anyone or anything too permanently. And that even included New Orleans.

During my hitchhiking excursions over the past few years I had seen enough of Texas to make me want to see some more. I had been hearing about a new music scene that was starting to emerge in Dallas and Houston and Austin. I wanted to find what that was all about.

An acquaintance, a guy named Rick Tracy, was planning to drive to Dallas. A few days after Thanksgiving, I piled my belongings into his big Lincoln.

Then it was time to say goodbye to Barbara.

"I love you."

"I love you, too."

"I gotta do this."

"I know."

She surprised me with her solid acceptance. "You're used to women crying when you leave," she said. "I'm not going to cry."

We had a great passionate goodbye, standing there on her porch. Then I was off to Texas, to see what it held for me and my music.

Two minutes later, I was back. Talk about anticlimactic.
"Have to take a leak."
Then, gone. For real.

"In Bed"

Chapter 4

The Rubaiyat in Dallas . . . A song that shaped my performances . . . Ramblin' Jack Elliot and his cowboy magic . . . From Austin to New Orleans and meeting Bojangles . . .

In those days, if you were into folk music and the like, and you lived anywhere near Dallas, you knew the Rubaiyat.

It was a theater-style coffeehouse, converted from an old garage. Held about eighty people. The place was run by an entertainer named Ron Shipman and his dad. Acts were mostly college students from the North Dallas area. Michael Murphey, Johnny Vandiver, Donny Brooks and others.

One night shortly after I arrived in Dallas, I walked in and drew a turn at playing. Next day, I found a room on McKinney Avenue not far away and began playing the Rubaiyat steadily.

I was now writing every day. One of the first of those songs born in Texas was "Little Bird." I always like to set the guitar out in a room in case I feel like picking. I woke up one morning, it was raining, and a little bird was on the windowsill.

Little Bird

Little bird come sit upon my windowsill
He sat there, through the falling rain
As I watched that little bird upon my windowsill
Saw those thoughts of you go by again

CHORUS
　　And the picture my face
　　Reflected on the pane
　　Is it tears I see or is it rain?

I remember how we talked before we said goodbye

A promotional shot from the late '60s. Perfecting the laid-back wandering minstrel lifestyle . . . kids, don't try this at home, leave it to the professionals.

Too young to know the world outside our door.
We laughed and said that love was free
Like birds that fly the winds.
And the rain today made me think of you once more.

CHORUS

I've no regrets about the past; I see how young we were
When the world was love and time was but a thought
But many things go many ways and many times but once
Till your life is past and your love is but a thought.

CHORUS

As my thoughts go tumbling back I wonder how you look
I wonder if you've seen that little bird
I wonder if he's sat upon your windowsill
And I wonder if you'll ever hear these words.

CHORUS

For years, "Little Bird" was the second song I would play at every performance. It was a special song for me, a first break away from the standards other folk acts were singing. The reaction of audiences to "Little Bird" and songs like it shaped my performances and helped me find my own approach.

Around that same time I also wrote "Driftin' Way Of Life," another early stab at creating a lyrical style of my own. The way it came about, Michael Murphey one night sang a gospel song with a melody that I liked. The next day I came back playing it with words of my own.

Driftin' Way Of Life

CHORUS:
> I'm singing about the driftin' way of life.
> It's different from the many that I've known.
> And every day I'll walk a strange new road.
> Hoo hoo hoo by myself
> I'll keep livin' it right or wrong.

> Well I've hitchhiked about a hundred thousand miles.
> I've had good luck and lived in different styles.
> But all the folks no matter what place or age,
> Tried to put me like a free bird in a cage.
> I've tied some knots with friends I'd hate to lose.
> I say we're friends because we give the right to choose
> But things get tight when your friends get out of place
> And try to change your big hat or shape your face.

(Chorus)

> Now in my mind you know I thought of settlin' down.
> Stop my roamin', forget this bangin' around
> But to live my life among groups every day
> Will either change me or send me on my way.

(Chorus)

> And as it stands, I'm never down and out too long
> 'Cause I kiss the blues goodbye with every song
> And I'm living my life as it feels to me right now
> And there ain't nothing in this world can hold me down.

(Chorus)

As in New Orleans, I was living for music, listening and learning, picking up bits and pieces that fit with what I was trying to do. Donny Brooks could play harmonica like wind blowing through the bluebonnets. He was just a kid, but he was pouring out sounds, mournful and joyous. I had that neck-mounted rig for my own harp, but Donny was the real goods. We would swap techniques and play off one another.

Patch-pocket jeans, flowered shirt . . . remember those fabulous '70s? I wouldn't be surprised if my guitar case back then had a "Disco Sucks" sticker on it . . . disco does still suck, by the way.

André Szuch, a Hungarian refugee who landed in Texas, hung his paintings in the Rubaiyat and invited me to his place where he proudly poured short glasses of homemade wine. André loved to toast the gypsy life.

He'd say, "No truth like wine truth."

He was drawn to me because he knew I was free to roam. He'd play sad Gypsy music on his accordion. He painted to relax. A true Bohemian spirit.

He had been swept up in the 1956 revolution when Hungarians rose up to throw off the communist regime. André had come to the United States seeking freedom but found himself baking bread in Dallas for the seven years needed to earn his citizenship.

André had hitchhiked around Europe in his youth with a spoon in his boot for opportunity meals, a backpack as his hotel. He told us about free universities where a student could travel from town to town and just take a course while passing through in the summer.

We'd drink all the wine, tell all the stories, and André would toast me.

"Je-ree . . . you dahmn gypsy. You come and go as you please. You don't know how lucky you are."

Another character from the Rubaiyat was Segal Fry. Segal could pick and sing in an easy style and he befriended all the musicians in the Dallas and Houston areas. He was also friends with Ramblin' Jack Elliott. Ramblin' Jack came to town and stayed with Segal and played a couple of shows.

Watching Jack perform, I felt I was watching the real deal. He wove stories through his songs. He had been places, done things, lived life, and I felt the words of his songs meant more because of this.

Ramblin' Jack was a true rounder. Mischief-eye smiles and puckish humor. Just past young. Handsome. Always getting into some sort of mild trouble. Jack had been born Elliott Charles Adnopoz in Brooklyn, son of a dentist. But he grew up reading the western tales of Will James and was swept away into dreams of being a cowboy. At nine, Jack went down to the old Madison Square Garden. The rodeo was in New York City, and he went and hung around the chutes, trying to talk the cowboys into letting him ride the bulls of 1940.

"Run away from home when I was thirteen," he tells it. "Joined the rodeo. J-E Ranch Rodeo."

Jack was cowboys, cowboy music, folk songs. In 1951, he started hanging around with Woody Guthrie, awestruck. And Woody swept Jack right along with him as they hoboed and hitchhiked all over America.

Ramblin' Jack learned to subtly mimic the cowboys he worshipped. When he hit the West, the transformation was complete. He walked that ambling cowboy walk, smoked the handrolled, and was genuinely perfect-cowboy shy.

Among strangers, Jack was, and is, a quiet man. But when he gets to know you, you can't shut him up. And when he speaks he is all cowboy. Soft voice, a gentle direct crispness. His mouth, held just so, barely moving as he speaks.

Ramblin' Jack became a walking preserve of cowboy lore, stories and songs. The American ranch cowboy, the rodeo cowboy, the singin' cowboy, the little boy who dreams of bein' a cowboy — he was all of them. He sang about a West and of cowboys we've never actually known, but have felt.

Felt somewhere in the chest, about heart-high.

Jack would start playing a song, then he'd pause, talking and endlessly strumming as the story and the song blended into one rambling yarn. Then he'd sling his guitar on its strap around onto his back so both hands would be free to explain, "Y'see." Then he'd bring his guitar around front rapidly for a single strum of a chord.

That's what Ramblin' Jack Elliott taught me as I watched him inside the Rubaiyat. How to put magic and imagination into a song. How to touch strangers in the audience and put their souls in a cowboy heart on a midnight horse.

"Sitting on bed in hotel room"   I was still learning how to do it, but it dawned on me after watching Jack that it was easier to do what Woody Guthrie did, which is to have experiences and write about them. Easier to do that than go out and say, "Woody Guthrie did this." So I just figured I'd do what Woody Guthrie did.

Drifting in and out of people's lives allows you to keep changing on the go. I would not be tied down. I've got dust on my boots.

Allen Damron was one of the regulars appearing at the Rubaiyat. He told me, "You've got to see Austin. You need to go down there with me."

I said, "OK, let's do it."

Austin sure was different from Dallas. Gentler. Green Hill Country on one side, black-earth farms on the other. The University of Texas stood north of a prideful state capitol building. And somewhere off San Jacinto Street was this little coffeehouse run by a guy named Bill Simonson.

The place was called the id. The décor was as spare as its name.

The basic decoration was darkness. One room, about fifteen feet by thirty. You performed on a stool in simple crude spotlight. It was literally an empty space where people sat around and sang folk music.

I sat on the stool in the spotlight and played to the audience curled up on the floor, faces turned up and telling me with their eyes that I was connecting with them. I was playing for tips again. Passing the hat to students with enough money for a cup of coffee and not much else.

I was sure in need of a couch to stay on. A photographer named Jay Verhulst was taking photos for the id coffeehouse, and he said I could stay at his place. So I spent some nights there with Jay and his wife Pat, a graduate student in English at UT.

Over the next few months I was in and out of Dallas and Austin, working whatever clubs and roadhouses I could find. Walking into that fine spring of 1965. Out there on the highway, trying to grab a ride. A little satchel that looked like a doctor's medical kit in one hand, guitar case in the other. Cowboy hat, jeans, and a thumb out.

The next time I came through Austin, the id was gone. But the owner had opened a bigger club on Red River Street that became known as the 11th Door. This place clung to a steep hill, people entered the back door and walked down these dark stairs, down into the atmosphere of a basement club, though it was actually just a street-level storefront. Austin was still dry, so the menu was coffee and fruit drinks.

The 11th Door had a little more room than the id, and it paid money. Yep, fifteen or twenty dollars a night.

My first set, first night, I played "Little Bird" from Dallas, "Gypsy Songman" about New Orleans, "Driftin' Way Of Life" about everywhere in between. I played 'em my best.

There's no feeling to compare with laying your work in front of people and seeing it grab them. And that's what happened. As I played, the room seemed to stop. It was dead quiet except for me and the Angel. So still, it almost seemed the folks out there had stopped breathing.

And then, the applause.

Oh yeah. I liked Austin.

*   *   *

By now I had a bunch of songs that I was proud of, and I wanted to see them published.

In New Orleans I had met a Tulane grad student, Jay Edwards, who was devoting his spare time to collecting folk songs. He and his wife, Anne, and another Tulane student named Charles Lee Sens, would hang around coffeehouses jotting down songs, including some of mine.

I couldn't read music, sure couldn't write it. So Jay and Lee would sit and listen to me play, then transcribe each song.

They eventually published "The Coffee House Songbook," which included three songs I had written and was singing. They were credited to Jerry Ferris because that was how they all knew me at the time.

Those songs had been written before my reunion with my family, a time when Oneonta memories were trying to scratch their way out.

Dust On My Boots

I started traveling, my mind to unravel,
A footloose tramp I thought I'd play.
Now the knot's unwound, gal.
I'm singing a different song now.
Don't believe I'll ever change my way.

Cause I am a rambler, Love, youth I've gambled.
In songs I sing the rambler's blues.
No use in taking heart gal, ain't in my cards now,
Can't kick the dust off my boots

I figured there would be even more interest in the uptempo, livelier music that I was writing in Texas. Jay Verhulst and Lee Sens had helped me compile a lot of that newer work into the draft of a songbook, "Dust On My Boots." I wanted to see it published, just my songs, under the name of Jerry Jeff Walker.

I headed back to New Orleans to look up Jay Edwards.

It was sometime in the late spring of 1965. I felt as if I'd been gone for years, but as soon as I hit those streets, it all came flooding back.

I found where Barbara Lyons was living, down on Burgundy across from Cosimo's. Turned out that she had a new boyfriend. Within days I had pretty much discouraged him and fell in with Barbara like we'd never been apart. The boyfriend left, bound for Big Sur.

To find Babe, I walked down to Johnny Matassa's bar, that little joint where Babe bought paisano. They steered me to him.

Before long, I was back playing the streets as if I had never left.

But with one big difference. This time I was a songwriter for real, the work pouring out. I was writing from my own life and knowledge, and always looking for an experience or an emotion that I could use as the starting point for a new song.

Late one night — almost dawn during the Fourth of July weekend of '65 — I hit the big bonanza.

I was whistling along Decatur Street in a Sebastian Dangerfield mood when I met a beautiful girl on the sidewalk in front of Café du Monde. I turned to her as she walked past.

"You are so beautiful. I could love you the rest of my life."

She stopped right there and slowly rotated back toward me, coldly replying, "Now, that's a big crock of shit."

"Don't mince words. Tell me what you really feel."

"You're drunk," she said. (She was right about that.) "And that's just a come-on line."

"Don't you believe in love at first sight?" I said. "The possibility that you can see someone and know instantly that this could be it?"

"It hasn't happened lately."

"You're not really trying," I told her. "Wait a minute, let's get somebody to testify to true love."

I stepped into the open air Café du Monde and walked up to a young couple seated at the first table.

"How about you, young man? Stand up and defend my right to tell this beautiful lady that there is true love at first sight."

He blushed. The two of them giggled. I took one of the empty chairs from their table and climbed up on it, preaching in the darkness.

"Who in this whole place will stand beside me and testify that love at first sight is alive in this world?"

The only person standing near me by that time was a waiter telling me to get down before there was trouble.

"Love will not be threatened by force or doubt," I told him.

I turned back to the restaurant customers, "Who will proclaim that love is alive tonight in the French Quarter?"

"I would love for you to get down off that table," came a voice from the darkness of Decatur Street. Officer David Glaudi and his partner, Ferdinand Marziale, stood with arms folded.

"How about you, sir?" I reached out to the men in blue who were slowly walking toward me. "Here's your chance. You've been summoned to defend my right to tell this girl that I love her."

"Down. Right now."

The policemen were not apostles of love this night. I guess I didn't move quite fast enough, because the next words I heard were, "You're under arrest."

Into the back seat of the patrol car, escorted by my two blue angels. I glanced back as True Love stood on the curb of Decatur by the Café.

She crossed her graceful arms, looking like she might be saying, "See, I told you that you were wrong."

Then the fingertips of her right hand fluttered a little goodbye wave. I winked back, and was gone, down Decatur into the night.

A few blocks away, at the old First Precinct jail on Rampart, the desk sergeant logged me into jail as a 42-22, drunk in public.

The cell door shut. Eyes viewed me warily from the dimness inside.

Over in a dark corner, sitting in a spot of light, was a little pile of clothes arranged around the frail body of a spindly old man. He patted the bench beside him.

"Sit here if you want, kid. I won't bother you."

His face was peaceful. His clear eyes sparkled with kindness. He smiled a little hesitant smile, dragging a gnarled hand through what little hair he had, which was dirty and yellow-white.

"We're all gonna be here a while," he said. He seemed to be talking from experience.

"We can stare at the floor and watch time drag on. Or we could amuse ourselves. Just talk about what we've done. Where we've been. It'll make the time pass a little easier."

He started telling a story about a girl he loved once. Said to me, "You ever been in love?"

"Just tonight."

"No, not like that. I mean real love. Where it changes your life. Makes you want to be a better man. Makes you feel stronger as you face life. Like you've got someone to share everything with. That kind of love."

"No, afraid not."

He began to tell about marriages and divorces and good breaks and bad ones. "The whole fiasco."

He laughed as he spoke, relishing an audience.

When he heard my tale about Café du Monde, he said, "I'll testify to true love and love at first sight. I say take love any way you can find it and run with it as long as it holds."

I listened to his life. A life spent drifting, poor and searching. He followed minstrel shows early on and sold **"On table in Café du Monde"** door-to-door. Now he was hustling drinks and tips as a New Orleans street dancer.

"I had a dog. Great dog." His eyes welled. "Best friend for a lot of years. Part of my act.

"We were doin' pretty good. I'd bought a two-hundred-dollar convertible to travel in.

"We were in West Texas at a truck stop, gassin' up, when a woman in a car pulled in across the highway, a lap dog in her front seat, yappin' away. My dog jumped out of the convertible, making a beeline for that doggie." He told it with eyes staring straight ahead.

"Wham. Car hit him. Killed him dead. Saddest day of my life."

He sat there shaking his head. I realized he hadn't been near this torn up telling me about any of his ex-wives' departures.

About this point we were deep into ourselves, and one of the guys in the cell jumped up and said, "Come on, Bojangles. Give us a little dance."

Lots of street dancers, especially in New Orleans, called themselves Bojangles. They'd step in a door and say, "Bojangles here" and hit their taps on the floor to see if anybody was interested.

"Bojangles" wasn't so much a name as a category of itinerant street entertainer known back as far as the previous century.

The old man said, "Yes. Hell yes." He jumped up, and we all started clapping a rhythm, and he began to dance. *Clickety click click clickety click*. We were all grinning.

I spent much of that long holiday weekend talking to the old man, hearing about the tough blows life had dealt him, telling him my own dreams.

Finally, with the holiday ended, I found myself standing before the judge.

"Ten bucks or ten days."

I paid.

As I was leaving, I looked back at the line behind me and got a glimpse of the top of the little man's head.

Then out the door. I never saw him again.

Back on the street, I couldn't get that old man out of my head. His dancing, his sad stories, his dog.

I stuck around New Orleans through the end of August, playing the streets again. But as days went by, it began to seem more like a job than the joy it had once been.

My first weeks and months in the Quarter, I had seemed to run into fresh new experiences every time I turned a street corner. Now those adventures seemed to be increasingly rare. I found myself spending my days and nights doing what I had already done before.

I had gotten word that a music publisher in New York was interested in publishing my songbook, "Dust On My Boots." I told Barbara I was going to be leaving soon. We went to a big rolling, drunken, house party. After awhile, Barbara got tired and walked alone to her new apartment on Chartres. And when the sun started coming up, I walked out of the Quarter and headed for New York.

Chapter 5

The Village scene . . . Writing 'Mr. Bojangles'. . . Deep thoughts on love . . . 'By the time I make my million, they'll have a coin for it' . . .

Mom:

This is the ramblin' son here. I'm in New York City now for a bit. A lot has happened since I last saw you all. I played Texas and Colorado this past winter. Got me a new guitar and some new clothes.

I'd planned to be on a boat for Europe long ago but some interesting complications have arisen in the meantime. I am traveling and looking and trying to remain "unweighted-down" to be able to move and adopt all that I see that is good in my "road" philosophy. Well, some songs of my own creation have sprung out of this hashing out (about twenty-five going on thirty now). The people of Texas and Colorado encouraged me to try to do something with them.

The songs are much more <u>me</u> than just songs per se . . . The songs were created in an unwinding sense in a hope to communicate with people about people and places to get a better understanding of each other. The communication of peoples (or the lack of it) is probably the major frustration of our whole lives. (As we, the family, for one, can testify.) These aren't <u>great</u>, overpowering, works of philosophic importance, but put together with all that is written and said it becomes an added factor to understanding people and our times . . . .

I hope I didn't startle you or irritate you with the drunken birthday call from Texas (a present from the owner I was playing for at the time). I got a little nostalgic and wanted to say hello . . .

I've talked about myself quite a bit here but this is something I've tried to do with you and Pop quite often. It's something I couldn't do last fall because of the situation and the frame of mind

I was in coming back to get the Guard straight. I could not be jumping up and down, carrying on about what I had found so good for me on the road and then be willing to stay and "pay my debt" to society. I had resigned myself to do the job of straightening out the home scene. No thoughts about moving on again if it got better until I had brought things up to date.

One of the significant things about coming back, for me, was that it showed everything must and does move on. That is the exact reason I've had such a hard time writing you about what I'm doing and where I am at with myself. I've moved on, broadened, and I guess widened the gap. But it's good, damn good . . .

Life is a big, wide, wicked, nasty, wonderful, complex, simple, glory, gory place . . . A lot will crumble and change but what stays...ah, what a truth that is. This is what I am approaching now. This is not a theory that I have calculated. This is a living, working, growing me. As I found, I incorporated. This is me. Up till now. This what I sing. This is what I represent . . .

Till I knock on your door

your son

When I got up to New York I went straight to the Village and hooked up with Ben and Linda, who were living in a Manhattan apartment. Before long, Babe, Marc Ryan and Bob Fisher came through on another run at the clubs in New York and Boston.

Marc and Bob took Babe over to Gerde's Folk City for "Hoot Night." This is a night when every NYU student who thinks he plays "folk music" can get on stage and "do his thing."

I asked Babe how it went.

Babe says, "Well, Jer'uh, I puts my name on the list, and I'm sitting backstage waitin' for them to call on me. After looking around I'm thinking, 'If I can't play no better than some of these boys I'd as soon stayed home.'"

Babe shakes his head then says, "Well, they calls my name and I walks out there and takes a seat. I only get three songs, so on the third one I throw the guitar up behind my head and dance around on stage. I don't think they've ever seen that before because they really started clapping.

I thought, people have gone every Monday night waiting for the real thing, and here it is! Babe Stovall, in his Civil War coat, from Franklinton, Louisiana, playing his silver National guitar up behind his head, dancing to "Time Is Winding Up."

No wonder they were excited!

After Babe and Bob Fisher headed back south, Ben thought it was time for us to drop some acid.

He had acquired some LSD. Little tablets, enough to enlighten some, terrify others. Ben and Marc had already sampled the wares a few days before. I put the little tab on my tongue, and Marc Ryan steered me out the door, telling me, "Now we're gonna take you down to the Village and show you a good time."

All the crazy colors. Giggling. Peering in the alleys. Gazing at the panorama of insanity. I just kind of kicked back, chuckled to myself. One of me told the others of me, "Maintain dignity, roll with the flow."

And flow I did, more or less.

After a few weeks of New York City, I realized the book deal was bullshit, and I decided to head out, figuring to make my way down to Texas with a few stops in between. I was a road warrior now. I didn't even have to think about it. I made it to Columbus with more money than I started with. A couple of days' run. Piece of cake.

I drifted over to Kansas City and played a couple of nights at a club called the Vanguard, where a singer named Pete Troutner opened for me. Pete was ready to try the road too. We eased off one day in his car and zipped down to Austin together. Pete was a most interesting companion. The ladies thought Pete was beautiful, inside and out. He was a wild man, brilliant and easygoing, uncomplicated and '60s-crazy.

The '60s were definitely cooking. Music was changing, civil rights marches were transforming society, the war and war protests were exploding, and marijuana smoke floated over Austin like the morning mist above Zilker Park.

We started hearing about Vietnam. Being that close to the campus at the University of Texas, the discussions were intense.

Hair was starting to get longer, and that made for an interesting tension in Austin, home of a vigorous strain of rednecks who were not known to welcome outsiders.

The streets were full of beer-bloated fraternity boys, strutting football players, roughnecks with red faces and huge hands. Rancher-hatted Cadillac-drivers would stalk the new creatures contaminating their fine Austin sidewalks, pausing even at green lights to zip down their electric windows and cuss at any guy in blue jeans walking with a satchel and guitar case whose hair dared touch his collar.

It seemed that grass was everywhere. In spite of the rednecks, Austin existed as a "stoned zone." Mighta been the students, mighta been just the time. Oh, I smoked it too, but not much.

Let's just say I tried everything and tried it again just in case I missed it. But mostly, my mind was into my music and that's pretty much where it stayed.

Pete Troutner and I swung into the Austin scene, no problem. We didn't work together, but did our own things separately. That way we also got two checks. Allen Damron was playing the 11th Door. He played banjo and had lots of color to give an audience. Stories and songs about things going on around Austin. We got to be pretty good friends and soon I had another place to crash. Allen lived close to the 11th Door, so we'd drift on over there real late and stay up till dawn, picking out music all night and talking.

A lot of those nights and early mornings, I'd be by myself, pickin' out new songs that were taking shape in my head. I would write them and try them out at the clubs to see how they felt to me and to see how the faces in the chairs felt about them too.

At the time I was reading a lot of Dylan Thomas, and I was really into the concept of internal rhyme. One night, all alone with my guitar and a big yellow tablet, I started to write. I was working on a song with internal rhyme. The events of the past few months were still swirling inside, along with the memory of folks I'd met in jail cells in Columbus and New Orleans. Scratched out a section here and there, fixed it as I went.

And it just came out.

Knew a man Bojangles and he danced for you . . .

And here it came, just sort of tumbling out, one straight shot down the length of that yellow pad. On a night when the rest of the country was listening to the Beatles, I was writing a six-eight waltz about an old man and hope. It was a love song.

Mr. Bojangles

I knew a man Bojangles and he'd dance for you
In worn out shoes.
With silver hair, a ragged shirt, and baggy pants
He did the old soft shoe.
He jumped so high, jumped so high
Then he'd lightly touch down.
Mr. Bojangles, Mr. Bojangles, Mr. Bojangles, dance

I met him in a cell in New Orleans.
I was down and out.
He looked to me to be the eyes of age,
And he spoke right out.
He talked of life, he talked of life.
He laughed and slapped his leg a step.

He said the name Bojangles
And he danced a lick 'cross the cell.
He grabbed his pants, a better stance,
Then he jumped up so high.
He clicked his heels.
He let go a laugh, oh he let go a laugh.
Shook back his clothes all around.

(Chorus)

He danced for those at minstrel shows and
County fairs throughout the South.
He spoke with tears of fifteen years
How his dog and him traveled about.
His dog up and died, he up and died.
After twenty years he still grieves.

He said I dance now at every chance
In honky-tonks for drinks and tips.
But most o' the time I spend behind
These county bars, hell I drinks a bit.
He shook his head and as he shook his head
I heard someone ask him please

(Chorus)

I sat back and looked at what I had written. I thought, yeah, that's him.

In a lot of ways, Mr. Bojangles is a composite. He's a little bit of several people I met for only moments of a passing life.

I'd done a few rounds in jails and drunk tanks during the past year. I'd met a bunch of guys in jail and on the streets. And I met one very gentle old man in particular.

He's all those I met once and will never see again and will never forget.

That old man in New Orleans' First Precinct jail. The street singers and dancers, tapping loose shiny shoes and blasting harmonica, guys with names like Harmonica Slim, Pork Chops, and Skeet Pete and Repeat, plus names I barely remember.

Shadowy faces in the night under balconies with one bare lightbulb above, casting magical patterns around in the glow.

Yeah. That was him.

That was Mr. Bojangles.

There's actually another verse written that night in Austin, a verse I never play. His mentioning three wives and a circumcision and other things. I couldn't fit it all in. That's why I left it out.

I worked on it some more, alone, for a few days, and then it was done.

It became part of my growing song list. I worked it into my performances, refining it. One night when I was playing, a bunch of people came walking down the stairs into the stone walls of the 11th Door. One of those people was Sam.

Sally Ann Mitchell: S-A-M. Tall, regal. Classy in a warm, friendly way. And beautiful. She was a rich man's daughter from Cincinnati, driving a '63 blue Corvette, her long blonde hair rippling in the wind around the roll bar. But what drew me to her was the way she carried herself, the way she talked, and the way she thought with a brilliant clarity.

Part of it was being young, part of it was the tenor of the times when we'd talk until the early hours. About the world, and what we thought it should be. Sometimes it was silence, when we'd just sit in the same room and tune our hearts to the same rhythm of life. We were two extremely independent people but we instantly became friends, and Sally and I were soon in love.

We were together as much as we could be when I was in Austin. Sally had a big, airy, old L-shaped house out by the railroad tracks west of downtown Austin, down in the funky area. Big back porch. It was my home for a time.

The quiet time of early Austin mornings. Few loud parties, no big booze or grass bouts. We were friends who wanted to talk, to share ideas, listen to music, pick some. We were working on our minds and spirits.

Walking out of the apartment at dawn, walking under those pecan trees, across those beautiful lawns next to the Capitol with a big lanky dog named Fawn. Just walking, being quiet together.

Sally and I had a great friendship. She often said that it wasn't just sexual, but spiritual. We had our hearts tuned to the same key. Sally had a coolness, a calm, a center. I respected her.

We really didn't talk much about marriage. Sally was very anti-marriage. And she was worried that her patrician father would have a fit if she showed up at the doorstep with an itinerant musician. Suited me; my feelings about entanglements were no secret. So instead of tying each other down, we did what a lot of married couples should do. We settled for fondness. It was spiritual, romantic, happy and euphoric. We both felt incredibly loved.

Every man should feel this close to someone. A purity and honesty of feeling. If you're the kind to leave it one day, you may still find other loves, even greater. But you also find that real love never ends.

Sally went to Europe, and I missed her. I sat down and scratched out the words to a song — the melody came later. "Morning Song to Sally" was something I felt as much as wrote.

Morning Song To Sally

As the morning light stretched in across m'bed
I thought of you
Remembering your laughing eyes and all we said
I love you too

And as all my thoughts of you
Pass 'fore m'face a thousand times
The way they race my heart
I cannot say it all in lines

How a short time together lasts so long
Makes me strong
As two weeks came and went
then you and I were gone
Living on

For it seems our love was destined
To be caught in other nets
But the love we held so briefly
I'd chance again without regrets.

We kissed goodbye so smooth it turned me 'round
'Round and 'round
But our cool sometimes returns to put me on
And slightly down
For we each have things to do before our time is done
But these thoughts of you here down the line
Prove a love has just begun.

Standing by that road has been my song before
Much too long
But now somehow I'm forced to see me there once more

And that's this song
But my waking thoughts of you are just extensions of my dreams
Without you here beside me I'll never know all that they mean

(Repeat first verse)

*   *   *

About that time Jay Verhulst was hired to run this bar near the state Capitol building, a real redneck hole, the Clown's Den. Notorious place, prone to the violent resolution of disputes. Even the best customers were rough.

Pete Troutner and I were in there one afternoon, shooting pool with some of the locals, when a stranger got up to audition for Jay.

Now, this was one different fella. Dark, stocky, intense. Looked like a young heavy-browed Beethoven wearing a '60s version of a zoot suit, Beatle boots. Playing a beat-up, nylon-string guitar and doing original material. The epitome of a New York City jazz player, he was Bob Bruno.

And he was good.

Bruno could play a wide range of instruments. Piano, valve trombone, string bass. He had been playing at the Iron Gate Inn, working a shift starting at four in the morning until the breakfast crowd rolled in for dawn burritos and beer. So Bruno, a proud jazz musician, was trying out for a job.

If there's a word used to describe Bruno and his music, it was genius. While genius does not buy food, it did allow him to pick up a guitar, which he seldom played, and try to write songs like the ones being sung in the protest movement and in the pop music of the day.

Pete and I stopped shooting pool, put down our cue sticks, found a table, and listened. Bruno had a biting sense of humor and a real awareness of the moment.

"I don't really want this gig, but I need it" and "I'm trying to be nice, but I'm dying inside" kind of stuff.

Since we were the only ones paying attention, Bob eventually came over to our table. He told us where he played and asked us to drop by.

In coming weeks we spent more and more time together, stayed up late playing the stuff we were doing.

Bruno asked if I was happy playing solo.

"I'd like to work up some of my songs, but I've never been in a group," I said.

We started jamming and playing on each others songs. We sang harmony together. Pete was best at harmony. I guess Bob's attraction to me was that I could work an audience, be personable.

He was too honest. If he was unhappy he told you.

We each kept playing our own gigs as we worked on song ideas we could share if we became a band.

We drifted towards Houston. I'd been playing a club called The Jester and knew that Houston, being a bigger city, had more places to work. Band gigs were more plentiful for sure. We weren't a band yet, but there we'd meet more musicians and have more opportunities to interact.

Guy Clark offered us a place to crash on the second floor of an old building he was using to build guitars.

Guy is an easygoing man with the strong convictions of a son raised by a small-town lawyer in Texas. Right and wrong are very clear to him. Folk music and song-writing gave him a great way to express how he felt about life.

He hadn't put all this together yet in 1965 Texas, but he had all the pieces ready to start. He was a strong stage performer. He could finger-pick with the best of them. He chose solid material, and he was dabbling in guitar-building.

He marched to his own drummer.

His best friend was Townes Van Zandt, a brooding, solemn poet who was starting to write.

We all found things in each other to admire.

Townes and I discussed songwriting once, and I asked him if he was committed. He said he was torn between his marriage, his family and school.

I said, "You gotta blow everything else off if you really want to do it."

"Jeff, I don't have that much time," he said.

I said, "Time as we know it?"

He nodded his head like he knew what I meant.

Guy introduced me to Gary B. White, a burly sort of a rascal who can bitch and complain with the best of them.

Gary once said to me, "By the time I make my million, they'll have a coin for it."

Gary played bass in an R&B band and banjo and guitar in a folk group while work-ing at NASA to make ends meet. He couldn't believe Bob Bruno, Pete Troutner and Jerry Jeff Walker were for real.

We'd fight and laugh and talk about recording as a band when we couldn't really play together very well. We did have some interesting songs, though. And I guess Gary knew he could help us, give us a solid foundation as bass player.

Gary started hanging out with us on the second floor of that apartment on Fannin Street. Bob started showing Gary more and more of our songs. It sort of felt like we were becoming a band.

But Bruno was getting impatient.

We also needed to make some money.

Chapter 6

Sixties music loud an' mean . . . An Irishman will break your heart . . . Janet, Jerry and the Lost Sea Dreamers . . . A gig in Carnegie Hall . . . Records and prosperity in New York . . .

The music scene was definitely changing. The war was escalating. Civil rights issues had gotten downright mean. A lot of people were dying for both causes. Realism was creeping into the love movement.

Looking back, I think people knew that before things would change, there had to be bloodshed. The resistance was deep, but the belief in what was right was just as strong.

We thought the war in Vietnam was wrong. That has been proven to be true.

We thought Richard Nixon was a crook. That has been proven to be true.

We thought that segregation was wrong, but we realized that that struggle will always be fought.

As a country, we stated right up front that all men were created equal, then we go and import us some slaves, kick the shit out of the American Indians, and then fuck with everybody in the Pacific Rim.

Bombs bursting in air and everywhere else.

Everybody in America now arms themselves and their children. To combat over-population our policy is probably, "Let 'em shoot each other. Then we'll have plenty of room."

The American drug policy of putting everybody in jail at the great expense of losing our freedoms is not working. To think a Third World country is going to stop selling a weed that grows in the parched soil just because we tell them to is a naive expectation at best.

The biggest drug problem we have is the way the government is handling it.

These were typical conversations at '60s parties.

Music in the '60s was getting meaner and louder.

Bob Dylan lyrics on top of Chuck Berry licks. The folk scene was changing. Things were costing more. Rent and drinks and bands themselves. Dylan was electric, and the Byrds had Top 40 hits with his lyrics.

Bruno and I would talk about this. He was coming from jazz. I was telling stories on a flattop. He was all improvisation. I was traditional. He didn't want to play anything the same way twice. I couldn't. We bumped heads. But we cared. Bruno held his emotions right out in front of you. He didn't hold anything back.

It was the right time to be working on becoming a band with all original material. This folk-jazz fusion thing was taking shape in our heads. We just needed to find people to help us make it happen, or maybe they'd find us, or maybe it would happen if we were in the right place.

But it started to dawn on us: looks like we're gonna play us some rock and roll.

Well, we had my songs, Bruno's songs, a few Buddy Holly tunes and some of the Beatles' stuff. Bruno was a musical genius. He could play anything.

We were starting to get a band together. Bruno on lead guitar, Pete playing tambourine and singing harmony. What the band needed was a name.

The Unhappy Frogs.

Bruno thinks we made the name up after smoking a lot of pot and doing word association. We let the first words that popped into our heads tumble out of our mouths. Well, that incarnation didn't last too long before we took another cue and gave the band a name which was an emblem of the times.

LSD . . . Lost Sea Dreamers. We were dreamers, all right. Also, the Lost Sea was where all those stolen guitars, lost sunglasses and broken promises ultimately wind up.

The new age called for new music. Loud rock music, psychedelic music. Album covers were starting to blossom with acid-inspired designs. The names of bands were often complex and bizarre. And the seeds were being planted for another band name that our strange flock of folkies and jazzmen and rockers would draw upon in just a few months.

We'd been to some girl's house. There was a bust. Folks were throwing stuff from a car when the cops moved in.

Busily, we went searching for it. Bruno found it. Mescaline. Naturally, we ate it on the spot. For some reason, we felt our next move had to be getting into this girl's back window.

So the bunch of us were boosting each other up, falling over, babbling encouragement, building impossible pyramids which collapsed under each other's weight.

Bruno laughed, flat on the ground. "Aha! The clowns of the Circus Maximus."

We were trying to get some gigs and a record, so we hooked up with a producer, a Houston lawyer named Gordon Bynum. He got an apartment for us. Bob Bruno, Pete and I moved in. But already, after the first few months of this, Bruno was getting pretty bummed out. He felt he was an improvisational jazz musician stuck with folkies who played the same thing over and over. Bruno stayed to himself much of the time. We'd all be out raising hell, and Bruno would be home alone. When we'd come in to crash, Bruno would be up, writing and playing by himself.

Bruno told us he'd had it. He was going home to Washington where he could get a job playing jazz. And I'd been thinking. What we all really needed to get things going was a record deal. So I told Bruno I was leaving with him. The two of us figured that if we were ever gonna be recorded, we either had to head to the East Coast or the West Coast. There was a pretty strong Austin-San Francisco connection going then — that's where Janis Joplin had headed. But Bruno was from Washington and I was from New York, and we just figured we knew the East Coast a little better.

There was this girl who'd been living with us, and she was taking off; she had a plane ticket to Mexico. Before she left, she gave us her car, an old Mercury station wagon. Just gave it to us. Only worth about seventy-five dollars.

Bruno and I cranked it up and left Houston with a couple of guitars and some of Bob's psychedelic paintings, his "falling through space on acid" stuff.

We were going to make New Orleans our first stop, but the Mercury seemed displeased with the prospect of becoming a band car. It quickly gave us a flat, no spare.

Right after we got that one fixed, we had another flat about 100 miles down the road. I figured New York must be fifteen or sixteen flats away.

We had about eight dollars left. I spent five of that to buy an old top hat, an Abe Lincoln top hat.

"Oh. Great, Jerry," Bruno rampaged. "You've got three dollars. Not enough left to buy gas or beer. But you've got a hat, though. Looks great with the cape."

Rock and roll called for a new image. I was trying on costumes.

Well, Bob had about twenty bucks stashed away, and we spent that on two cheap bald tires and made it to New Orleans. We looked up Barbara Lyons and stayed with her a couple of days to regroup and build up our cash flow. Good-hearted Barbara called a friend in Washington who sent us twenty-five bucks. We went out street-singing, made a little extra cash.

Bruno, the jazzman, somehow managed to grit his teeth through "Greenback Dollar," and we made five bucks and then he used that cash to hustle pool, making more money for our trip to New York.

Barbara and I said goodbye for the last time. I told her I'd fallen in love with her all over again during our stopover in New Orleans. But that only shocked her, because Barbara had been in love with me all along, and my words made her think. She wanted more. And she knew then that I was always going to be a drifter and that Irishmen will break your heart. Other road runners come along, love you and leave. But an Irishman, he has to convince you that he loves you.

Then he leaves.

That old Mercury rattled out of New Orleans, smoking and draggin' low. We tacked toward the north, slowly. Before we got up the coast we blew two more tires. But Bruno and I finally made it all the way to Washington, D.C., where we stayed with some of his friends.

Pete Troutner flew up to Washington and joined us. We were a trio with harmony, three guitars and a batch of good songs. But we needed a band. New York has more musicians than anywhere, so we figured, let's go to New York.

The Village was exciting right away. We parked the Mercury and stepped onto streets reverberating with the vibrant hippie era. Flutes on the sidewalks, long hair tied back with bandannas, barefoot beautiful women firmly jostling under colorful peasant dresses. Pungent smoke smells drifting down, air wafting with sitar music. Full blossoming wildflowers, years before those pretty young ones went to seed.

As ugly as that old Mercury was, she must have looked inviting to someone. That first night we were there somebody broke into the car and stole everything we had, including the instruments.

Welcome to New York.

They had stolen my guitar, Pete's guitar and left behind Bruno's old Mexican gut-string.

"Hey, why didn't they steal my guitar? What's wrong with my guitar?" Bruno boomed.

We had to laugh. "Because your guitar sucks."

Standing there on the sidewalks of New York with an empty shitty station wagon, virtually no money and little hope.

"Look," I told Bruno, "There's no use stayin' here. We've got no money and no music. Let's do something quick and try to get this goin' again."

We split up. Bruno, to Washington to work some jazz places. I went back to Houston, borrowed a guitar, and picked up a few hundred bucks playing at Sand Mountain coffeehouse.

It wasn't the cleanest season for us. While I was in Houston, Gordon Bynum set up a little recording session for me. We taped a few of my songs, including "Mr. Bojangles," which ultimately became quite a problem for me due to issues of who owned the rights to the song.

And things weren't going great for Bruno in Washington, where he was paying the rent by wiring new homes. That was a bit of a problem, since Bruno knew absolutely nothing about electricity.

Gary White was still in Houston, and I persuaded him to join us. Maybe get all his shit stolen, too. The two of us piled into his tiny sports car and drove through a cool, drizzling rain to Washington.

Gary and I rented a strange little house in the Washington suburbs. Actually, it was a cinder block hut way out in the woods over by Riverdale, Maryland. One of the first things we had to do was round up enough money to have propane gas delivered so we could heat the place. The nights were starting to get cool there in the fall of '66.

Bruno lived with relatives in the suburbs; Pete Troutner and his wife, Lynn, moved over from Kansas City.

The Lost Sea Dreamers went looking for work. And I sat in the freezing concrete shack and wrote letters back home.

Mom & Pop & Gram

Got the money you sent. Thanks again. We ate it to good use. Let's just think of this as a cheap college education. Books and tuition. I'm becoming a Road Scholar.

Anything I try that's involved with the group is always about twice as hard than if I were doing it by myself.

I got a house (cheap) that we can make noise in and practice as often as we want. Bob's mother gave us a rug, a couple of hide-a-beds and a chair & curtains.

We have Bob's record player and all our instruments here too, so we're pretty comfortable.

We're practicing as often as we can. Now that we're in the house (a couple of days) we should be on it every day. We have one record audition soon. Two agent auditions too. Gigs seem to be coming after New Years (everybody's got their bookings through the first). We have a lead on one place for a start. The Peppermint Lounge, of all places.

I don't believe I can make it for Christmas. It would be cheaper to stay here. We need to keep practicing and stay ready for work. Most of the money went for deposits and heat and rent. We're making it OK but any money for chow would be cool too.

Going to miss that Christmas dinner.

Ron

J. Walker
6601 Kenilworth Ave.
Riverdale, Maryland

We auditioned at the Peppermint Lounge using a guy from another band on drums, David Scherstrom. The gig was ours and David stayed on as our drummer. David was a baby-faced kid, eighteen years old, straight out of a high school "battle of the bands" mindset. He'd only been playing professionally a few months, and was in awe of our self-confidence to play our own material. But he jumped right in with us. It was good to have his youthful spirit.

The first gig was in two days, so we asked if we could lock our instruments and equipment in the basement until then. Hauling it around in Georgetown was difficult because of our car situation. They said, "Sure." So we left to celebrate getting some steady work.

The next day we got a call. The club had been broken into and our stuff was stolen. This time, we weren't waiting. The call went out to friends and family. We borrowed enough to just get something to beat on, some hack guitars and Dave's drums.

The Northeast in November and December is shitty. We were cold, broke and hungry. Waitresses and Bruno's grandma and mother would invite us to eat and we ate like it was our last meal. Our cinder block house was eating us alive in fuel bills. It was depressing.

We worked through New Year's and decided we would take the New York plunge. We had to position ourselves to be seen and heard. Through contacts at the Peppermint Lounge, we got a date at Cafe Wha? in the Village. So Gary White, Bob Bruno, Pete and Lynn Troutner, David Scherstrom and myself were New York-bound.

Now we had to make enough money to finance the trip. Try to make a little money playing so we could finally get to New York, where the gig would start ten days away.

We were playing one of those basement dungeon clubs of stone and wood that had been made popular earlier in the '60s. Down on the Potomac River, far away from the thin ties and slick suits of government Washington.

People who really liked music and bar nights gravitated there. The off-duty bartenders and waitresses would drop by, so it was becoming our place.

But tonight it was the early set, a rainy night. And two paying customers. One of them, this beautiful innocent girl sitting there staring up at me, her eyes wide, her chin in her hands, this knowing smile on her face. And I stepped down to talk with her during my first break.

Janet Forbes, twenty years old. Just about beautiful, just about tender. Wistful eyes, then and now. Eyes that look at horizons with the best of the cowboys and sailors and poets.

Navy brat, twenty homes before she was in the third grade. And in her childhood, her family finally settled just outside Washington, in Rockville, Maryland.

Janet had been working since her mid-teens. She was with a computer firm in Bethesda when I met her. She lived at home with her mother, her sister and younger brother. She was shy, straightforward, and ready to leave Maryland.

We talked about the band going to New York. Big move, get in the thick of it. Janet said it sounded exciting. She'd always dreamed of New York. Why didn't she go too? That's where the action seemed to be.

She also wanted to start thinking of herself, about what she wanted to do. She wondered how people just struck out on their own like that.

I told her exactly what Howie Clark had said to me when I sat on a bar stool in Oneonta yearning to get away: "You just do it. That's all. Or forget about it."

All this happened on a Friday night. I didn't know it, but I had exactly five more days to be a bachelor.

Janet and I hooked up immediately. For the next couple of days, I don't think we were apart for a minute. Two days after we met, we were walking into her place after a trip to the supermarket. She had groceries in her arms.

I looked at her and said, "You have any money? Real money?"

Janet didn't hesitate. "Yeah. I have several thousand dollars."

"You wanna get married? Go to New York?"

"Yes." With one word.

"World's Greatest Proposal," she called it.

But first we had to have a little talk. With all the passion of the past two days, Janet and I had not had time to cover all the particulars of our lives.

I sat her down on the couch and held her hand, with sad full eyes.

"Janet, I have something to tell you."

Her eyes got big and serious and a little fearful.

"My name isn't really Jerry Jeff."

"Oh? Oh. Big deal."

She handled that pretty well, I figured. She now knew she was going to be Janet Crosby, not Janet Walker. We got everything together for the wedding and the trip to New York. Janet's company didn't want her to quit, so they transferred her to the New York office. Good news, steady work when we got there.

We planned to get married at 10:30 Thursday morning. Well, "planned" is not exactly the right word. Thursday morning, we were camped outside a jewelry store waiting for it to open so that we could buy rings.

I was almost shouting at the glass cases, "Whattya got in wedding rings that match?"

"How much are they? What's the cheapest one you've got?"

"OK, we'll take those. They're fine."

The Rockville County Courthouse. January 26, 1967. The bride, Janet Bernice Forbes, now Mrs. Ronald Clyde Crosby. She had just turned twenty.

Her face was one of '60s innocence. She had dark, full eyebrows and a true smile across those eyes. Eyes that won't allow her to play cards for money or lie to someone she loves. She was excited, but she also didn't feel well. She'd been feeling poorly all week but running on adrenaline.

From the courthouse we went straight to a hospital, where Janet was diagnosed with bronchitis and put in an oxygen tent.

Life tends to set a fast pace at times.

Bruno was not happy about the marriage. In his blunt way he had been telling us, "Chicks break up bands. We don't need a chick singer. We have lyrics to sell our songs. The guys don't need to be sidetracked by women. It'll tear the band apart."

Now Pete was married, I was married, and David was engaged.

Right away, I had my first test of loyalties. We were due in New York for our gig. I felt a lot of pressure to show that the band came first, hold up my end of the commitment.

I guess that's the reason I left for New York. It may not have been right but it was a fact. I had to go.

I talked with Janet. She looked so lonely in the hospital bed. We would be together a long time, I told her. We'd get through it. We were married. And we would make it because we both wanted to be in New York. We both wanted to get out of Washington.

"I'll just go on ahead. You rest. I'll work the gigs, and Gary and I will find us an apartment. Pete and Lynn are going to find a place too. When you're stronger, I'll come get you and move you to New York."

With Janet in the hospital, the band and I piled all of our instruments and suitcases into a trailer behind Pete's old Falcon station wagon. Gary and I drove in his Triumph. We were away, following gray-rain freeways, north to New York, straight to the Cafe Wha?, where we were supposed to have a gig starting that night.

"Lost Sea Dreamers, who?" They'd never heard of us.

"Well, since you're here, let's have a listen."

We hauled everything out of the cars, set up inside and auditioned right there on the spot that very night. They liked us, put us in their rotation. Five bucks a man per set. We had a gig but no place to stay.

Gary knew a young couple in town and he and I slept on their floor. Pete, Bruno and Dave spent the first night freezing, sleeping in Pete's Falcon out by the curb.

We played the Cafe Wha? and I found an apartment for us on Thompson Street. Gary White still had his Triumph. We had to keep parking in different places to keep it from being towed.

That problem was solved when it, too, was stolen. Gary simply used the insurance money to get an apartment across the hall in the same building on Thompson.

Janet moved up, the other guys in the band still wondering where she had come from. So we all piled into the Thompson Street apartment, thanks to Janet's savings, the whole band sleeping on the floor that first week.

Bruno didn't want female distractions, but Lynn Troutner, Gail Scherstrom and "Janet Jeff" all helped the band make ends meet from time to time. It also gave us some home life away from the stage and the bars.

So there we were, the new family of the Lost Sea Dreamers, in the vital heart of the Village in 1967. Our place was at 231 Thompson Street, right above a first-floor beauty shop and barbershop. Just a small apartment building, fire escape out front, a short block away from Washington Square park.

The Village was a real neighborhood then, clubs going all the time on Macdougal and Bleeker, right around the corner. The streets were alive with people at all hours — like New Orleans, never sleeping.

Our place wasn't much. One big empty room up front above Thompson Street. Little bedroom in the back. Kitchen and the bathroom kinda jammed into a little alcove, the shower right across from the stove. Not much space, and not much in it. All for $110 a month.

We had a wonderful janitor named Armando. He helped us furnish our apartment by bringing us stuff left behind in other buildings.

He would knock on the door. "Jerrreee. You want a Louis XIVth chair?"

It would be a little rickety but it would do the job if you propped it in the corner.

Armando slept in the basement and bottled homemade wine and sang songs on a banjo that he later gave me. On the cover of the *Mr. Bojangles* album, I'm holding the banjo. And wearing the top hat Bruno hated.

When Armando gave the banjo to me he said, "You remember me."

I always will.

Just about an hour before dawn, I'd weave my way home from the clubs, the bold crow of a rooster in Manhattan calling the way. Chickens and taxi horns. Clucking, floating gently on the air above the distant subway rumble.

Armando the janitor, the Little Rooster. Armando took care of everything in our apartment, and took care of the people inside. And in the alley behind our place, Armando raised chickens in splendid violation of a broad array of city ordinances.

You'd wake up in your apartment, the window open. All of a sudden:

"Crawakadooooo"

The Thompson Street apartment was brimming with cockroaches. When you came in at night and turned on the light, the room shifted slightly with their bustle. You could almost hear tiny voices, like windstraw, calling out the alert.

Janet and I would get naked and arm ourselves with a couple of cans of Raid. Naked, so the cockroaches wouldn't climb up our clothes; cowboy boots so you could stomp 'em when they ran into the corners. And we'd run around the apartment, clomping in our boots, blasting the air with that oily spray, laughing and cussing. Pretty soon we'd scrape up a pile of dead cockroaches into the middle of the room.

The neighbors would holler at us, "Hey, you spraying for roaches again? My place is full of cockroaches running from your place. Keep your own share!"

Janet started to cook once we got the place tidied up a bit. We had spaghetti mostly. At first Janet thought a recipe calling for clove of garlic meant the entire clump. We noticed that the other guys seemed to move out quickly after that.

Janet and I lived in the apartment over the beauty shop, Gary lived across the hall over the barbershop. Frank's Physiognomical Haircutting had all these pictures of haircuts tacked up, looked like they were out of *Harper's Bazaar*.

Frank's was still there last time I looked. So were the magazine photos, updated of course. And sun-faded in the windows.

Livin' and playin' Greenwich Village. Cafe Wha? Lost Sea Dreamers. It was a fun time to be living there. Frank Zappa, the Fugs, Mama Cass, John Sebastian, James Taylor, all of them playing clubs right down the block.

There was music on the street at night, magic all the time. Hippies and street craziness. One of the creative centers of the '60s. And we were playing psychedelic rock right there, floating amid the soft fury of all that pot smoke. It never smells the same anymore, never seems quite that way again.

I was getting caught up in this transformation. I had bought an English bobby capecoat, still had the top hat, the mustache and lip broom under my lower lip. The Village was full of characters, and I felt like one. Boppin' around the Village in these little round sunglasses. Cape-coat. Pants tucked inside high boots. Top hat. Groovin' to my own drummer.

One day I stopped by the *Village Voice* lookin' like Scaramouch and ran smack into Don Brooks.

Yeah, Donny Brooks had moved from Texas to New York, bringing with him those beautiful harmonica sounds. He lived down at the end of the block. And it was quite a block. Paul Seibel and Emmylou Harris were living together right up the street. Townes Van Zandt would ease through every now and then. Didn't have to walk far to pick and sing with friends.

We played at the Wha? for about a week. Then we auditioned around the corner at the Night Owl, where James Taylor and the Flying Machine were playing and the Mamas and the Papas had been through earlier. The guy in the Night Owl said he'd pay us ten bucks a man, per night.

The Lost Sea Dreamers were the house band for the Night Owl for several weeks before all that ran its course and we were looking for work again. Gary read in the paper that a new place called the Electric Circus was opening. They were looking for a house band. We auditioned, and they loved us.

Our instincts for being in New York were turning out right. One night at the Night Owl, Steven Sondheim and Maynard Solomon (the president of Vanguard Records) wandered in after dinner for drinks. That got us an audition at Vanguard.

The studio was exciting but at the same time, disappointing. We had to learn a new side of the music business. Then we had to pay for mixing, and we had to join the union to get the album released, and that took all our advance money. We almost didn't put the album out because we needed the money for studio time, to pay rent and get some needed equipment.

Now the record company wanted to change our name. The bigwigs at Vanguard Records got talking with the music slicks at Electric Circus. And they figured that Lost Sea Dreamers — spell that *L-S-D* — was not the best image for their new club.

They suggested a name change, something to go with the theme of the Electric Circus. Well, Bob's idea from the year before in Houston, inspired by a hatful of mescaline and an unlawful entry, seemed fine to them. So the Lost Sea Dreamers became Circus Maximus.

We weren't wild about that but the record company wanted it, the club wanted it, and our new producer, Dan Elliot, wanted it. So the Electric Circus had 'em a house band, Circus Maximus. And Vanguard had a psychedelic rock band, most strange for Vanguard, which was a folk artist's preserve. But the label had just signed Country Joe & the Fish, and now we were Vanguard's second rock group.

It's funny, but all the years I was solo, I was writing songs and listening to folk acts on Vanguard. Now, I was signed by the label, and I was all electric.

We gave the Electric Circus our best. Room-storming rock and roll, real loud, hard, muscular rock and roll. But good.

We seemed to fit in with the bizarre avant-garde mixed arts theme of the club. Jugglers, clowns, fire-eaters. A guy who slid down a high wire to open the show. Karate presented as fine art with grace, powerful kata under strobe lights. The Lamp Man, who stood on stage as a pinpoint of light pierced his face, the light very slowly spreading to illuminate just his head as he progressively growled himself into a rage. That was his entire act. The Lamp Man.

Seven or eight light shows, seven or eight projectors, the whole place throbbing with sexual overtones, dancers. We had a band room, all foam rubber like stalactites, a strobe light the only lighting in the room. We'd pass a joint around.

With this creative surge, we went into the studio to cut our first album. The Vanguard studio, true to its highbrow heritage, was set up for orchestra. A sea of chairs in one big room. So they built this corkboard enclosure around us. Vanguard's tweedy studio felt the thunder of heavy amps jumping electric.

That album, *Circus Maximus*, came out in late 1967. Bob Bruno wrote seven of the songs on our first album, I wrote four. And our pictures on the cover, damn, we looked so young. Me with that long hair, black mustache and scraggly lower lip.

We cut that album at the Vanguard studios on a single Ampex four-track recorder. It was 1966.

We were raw, we were intense, we were broke. We tried. We were excited. We had no help. Dan Elliot could no more produce an album than I could fly. But we made the best of what we had. It was like pulling teeth, your own.

We hung around Israel Young's Folklore Center, a guitar store which dealt in guitars, banjos, dulcimers, twelve-strings. It had a lot of fine instruments and that array drew the finest pickers inside. Many of us, at the time, could only afford new guitar strings.

Don Brooks and I had stayed in touch and he called me up one day and said, "Hey, I got this guy you should meet who plays a little bit of acoustic music."

Yeah, that guy played a little bit of acoustic music, all right. Donny Brooks introduced me to David Bromberg.

Bromberg is the reason man created stringed instruments. David touched them with a lover's fingers and they moaned that true love right back at him. Wood and wire and flesh spoke.

The day I met David, we immediately sat down and played, right there in Donny

Circus Maximus

Brooks' apartment. Over time, it was music first, then friendship. The closeness let us share some dreams. We talked a lot about my days as a solo folk singer, and how that acoustic sound was still alive in my chest, softly speaking its poetry even though, at the time, I was wielding an electric guitar and deafening '60s youth in the Village while they fumigated their gray cells.

Right down the street from our apartment was the Kettle of Fish bar. Sawdust floors, eight or ten tables. That was our hangout, a creative exchange for artists in the afternoon heat or the vibrant cool mornings after closing time. We'd get together and play songs all night, stuff we were writing in our little apartments scattered in the Village. Hanging around tables racked full of bottles of beer and glasses of wine, sloshing and spilling in sloppy cadence with tapping feet. The best song we had ever heard was the one we had just played, usually.

"Kettle of Fish"

"Hey, I'm workin' on this one. Gimme the guitar, lemme show you what I've got."

Being writers. Finding the song, a poem, a proper silence. The words many folks just can't find by themselves. But they know when they hear our music that it's part of their soul, their bones, life and every past life they can feel. The way heaven's gonna be when we get there and someone whispers a song we knew all along but just couldn't, somehow, find the words by ourselves.

It's the smell of a woman's hair passing by. Or how a kid looks at you in a certain way, sharing a knowledge and remembered mischief. Or those strays we see on the side of the road. Stop the car, open the door and say, "OK. Git in."

Wish I could sing you a song tonight. When folks can't hear the words in their own hearts, sometimes those are the words I can free with my music. That trust between an artist and the fan. When they believe, trusting and sure, that the words they want to hear are mine.

The Kettle of Fish had those very folks, a room, a corner, a table with friends gathered up together, friends like Paul Seibel, Townes Van Zandt, Gary White, David Bromberg, Nick Holmes. Once, Ramblin' Jack dropped by, and I played "Mr. Bojangles" for him.

"Jack, it's gonna be a hit."

"Aw. Well. Yeah. But."

"But what?"

"Too many words in it. Strange words."

All this creative, flashing energy was exciting. It was lightning in the streets, rumbling energy in the bars, laughter with friends, and music.

We were sort of the third shift at the Kettle of Fish.

First shift, the old Italian men who called the Village their home. Caruso scratching out of the jukebox all afternoon. Venison cacciatore in the kitchen, one guy cooking for his buddies.

About six o'clock, second shift burst inside, the truck drivers getting off work. Furniture movers, talking about betting the horses, slamming their drinks fast and hard till they got drunk and left early because they got up early. About eight o'clock, the Village artists would drift in for the evening. Performers, broken down actors, magicians wafting under the grimy globes of ceiling lights. The sawdust would muffle our laughter and the spilling of beer.

When we weren't gigging, I was off with Bromberg, meeting his friends and trading songs. One night David and I were pickin' and drinkin'. We'd been up for hours, the crisp breath of November pushing through the window deep into our lungs.

David said, "Let's drop in over at WBAI. Bob Fass is on right now."

Bob Fass had a live program from midnight till dawn on WBAI, the Pacifica radio station in New York City, "listener-supported communist radio" one friend called it. Live music, new music, poetry, Pacifica's lively left-of-left political harangues. Bob Fass's live program was a musical reference point for the entire city.

David and I were pretty loose that night. I carried up a big 7-Up bottle, half soft drink, probably a little more than half Seagram's 7. We ambled in while Bob Fass hulked over his control board, his perpetually troubled face presiding over a tall, powerful, gentle frame. His voice, soothing as the wind-chime-in-the-background sound of late '60s radio.

I curled to the floor, my guitar against the wall, and went to sleep after the most modest of pleasantries. David nudged me awake, Bob Fass' rumbling baritone filling the crowded room. David and I began to play for him, live radio. We probably played from two in the morning until about five. Talked a lot with Bob, played some music, had a good time. David and I sat on the edge of cheap old chairs, leaning into the mikes. The room swelled with strings coaxing out a six-eight waltz. And I began to sing.

Knew a man, Bojangles and
He danced for you, in worn-out shoes . . .

And the radio played our song that night. On windowsills around Manhattan where only the lonely listen. In cabs dashing down the avenue, careening toward pedestrians. Beaded curtains in Tribeca shimmered at the melody washing over two lovers twisting on a couch.

Well, I was a little bit drunk and literally in tears. We were singing that long, long love song on midnight radio. Bob Fass was taping his show as we sang. He recorded the voice of a young man singing what sounded like an old song. Ageless. Something we'd all heard before and forgotten somehow, and were glad to hear again. The voice on that tape was pure, innocent, young. Not the gravel that would eventually come with age, but a fresh new brook over clean rocks.

When we finished that last verse, the strings slowed their humming to a whisper, the airways were silent a few seconds, then Bob Fass said: "That is a *beautiful* song. You wrote that?"

A few days later we heard the song on WBAI again. And again. And again. Bob Fass was playing that tape he'd made, and "Mr. Bojangles" was all over Manhattan. WBAI loved it and its listeners loved it. Sometimes Bob would play it three or four times a night.

While most radio stations stuck to a tightly regimented format and limited play lists of Top 40 songs, here was listener-supported, leftie-babble WBAI snatching a sound from the winds and playing it over and over to New York City, the nation's largest radio market.

I didn't know it then, but this would become the pattern of my career. When all the conventional avenues were closed to me, I'd just be walkin' down the alley singin' my songs. Record companies and big executives with honker cigars might insist I do it their way. But usually I'd be off on my own, playing music the way I like it. And folks who wanted to hear those songs would be with me.

With all that exposure from WBAI, people began showing up in record stores all over New York wanting to buy "Mr. Bojangles," which didn't exist as a record. The only recording of my song was the one that Bob Fass had taped when I played live on WBAI.

So some fat was in the fire that would continue to sizzle for several months. Right in the midst of this, something strange and wonderful happened with Circus Maximus.

The same year we'd crawled into New York City, the year of the stolen instruments, the cockroaches, playing for five bucks a night . . . that same year, Circus Maximus was booked into Carnegie Hall.

Seemed that a well-known psychologist had wandered into the Electric Circus one day and expressed astonishment at the similarities between our pounding psyche-delic rock and medieval French music. Somehow this resulted in an offer to play a joint performance at Carnegie Hall with the New York Pro Musica Antiqua. An evening of psychedelic longhairs and professorial longhairs. The Antiqua was devot-ed to the preservation of classical 13th-century pre-Baroque music, playing instru-ments constructed of wood, bladders and connective tissues. Instruments like the krummhorn and the sackbut. Bob Bruno, with splendid mind, took one of Pro Musica's ancient ditties and translated it into Circus Maximus acid rock. Centuries apart, we played with the confidence of our eras.

It was the Electric Christmas. Carnegie Hall, December 26 and 30, 1967. Heady stuff. Life was good. We stood on the wooden stage and looked into that cavern beyond the spotlights. The great red velvet forever. The awesome experience of feeling totally exposed, standing on a ledge of light.

December 1967

Hello Oneonta. Homeland of parenthood and soul.

This is the periodic reporting saying hello again from Manhattan. We still live at 231 Thompson St. (to answer the redundant cry of mother).

We are sending some pictures and records (in lieu of money). The album has been out about a month. I have been busy so I haven't sent something till now. Some money for grandmother and Christmas was my plan (with the records) but money will come in about a week or so.

We've been pretty poor lately, but things are changing now that the record's out (if you have a stereo record player the album sounds better, better mixes). I'm hoping to get tickets soon for a Christmas concert we are giving in conjunction with the Pro Musica Antiqua at Carnegie Hall. It is an evening with 13th-century folk musicians, a modern rock group and electronic music, all combined (yes we are poor but we are at Carnegie Hall).

I have written a song that was played first on a Manhattan station where I went and sang all evening. The song is "Mr. Bojangles." (The one about being in jail.) The song is played about three times a week, and I've gotten quite a few responses from it. Due to reasons I can't go into, we as a group, probably won't do it (not our image?). So I made a copy and through a man who loved the song very much I sent it to Nashville, Tenn. in hopes Marty Robbins might dig it and make us both some fantastic money on it. (I just sent it two days ago so it will take a while.)

We have started on our new album and it will be done in January. Release is March first. Single should be out in January before the album. We've gotten some good write-ups that say we're great and avant-garde, and the music agencies say we're not dumb enough for popular consumption.

Grandma,

I thought I would put a little message in with the money. First of all I want to say that we couldn't have gotten that first album out without your help. We probably would have gotten lost somewhere along the way. We had quite a bit of stuff stolen and at one point the "Haines" was the only guitar amp we had. We played both lead and rhythm through it.

Before December is over with I'll be making some more money

85

that I could send you. I wish you would tell me how much has been paid out already so I will have some idea of where you stand financially with the amp. I hope (I know) this will be a help at Christmas time. I am going to get tickets for you and Mom and Pop for the Carnegie Hall concert the 30th of December. Hope you can make it then. I'll call you soon on the phone.

Your grandson — Ronnie

The concerts rated mention in Time magazine and a Sunday spread in The New York Times. The newspaper reviewer was not kind: "Somewhere between the opening of a new supermarket and Times Square on Guy Fawkes Day."

Yet we had experienced great days of our young lives, key moments and elation.

Oh, and we were regularly getting not only our instruments stolen, but our cars.

"Down the stairs"

Gary lost his little car to the streets. It came back eventually but had that lopsided look of a cat which had been run over and never quite looked the same again. Pete's Falcon kept losing its essentials. A battery one day. Hubcaps the next. Can you imagine any possible value of Falcon hubcaps in the late '60s? And then, the final welcome, the pure acknowledgment that we were in New York City. One morning, the Falcon was just resting on its axles by the curb, somebody somewhere having been in need of four bald tires and rims.

About that time we were cutting our second album with Vanguard, *Neverland Revisited*, but there was a problem. The drummer. Dave Scherstrom's drum parts just weren't right. Finally, we brought in a session drummer, a guy we'd never seen before, Bill LaVorney.

The album didn't sound right. The band had split into two factions. Bruno huddled under black temperamental moods, trying to draw the band toward the more exotic free-form music which was his background. He and Pete sided together over the drummer. Gary and I not only had our doubts about the drum parts, we were also feeling the relentless draw of other music.

Bruno was saying, "I don't like our albums. I don't like either one of them. I don't think they're representative of our music. We played loud, raucous music. Not what this is, this is a studio parody."

Gary ambled over to me. "Bruno . . . he really is a genius. But he's so crazy he's hard to live with sometimes. He can't let things be, he always has to keep things exciting by keeping everybody miserable. He keeps putting on more and more pressure."

I just told Gary, "Hey, screw it, man."

Circus Maximus was still intact, although struggling. We had played Carnegie Hall, yet now we were back to dragging a U-Haul behind the old Falcon to get to our gigs. And we had no heart. I didn't want to sing, Bruno didn't want to sing, Pete would step up and beat the tambourine singing our songs so we could finish the gigs. We were arguing on stage.

It was time to conduct a healing ceremony. Ben Jennings came over from his place, to cook, to preside. Right away, I should have figured if Ben was in this, something momentous and possibly life-threatening was about to happen.

We threw open the doors to the hallway on Thompson Street, breezily wandering from Gary's apartment to ours, Janet and Jerry's. Ben and Janet had the kitchens going, cooking up mounds of hot Mexican food. Lots of food. Lots of food, tequila, beer, sangria, pot. Everybody was there. Bromberg, the band, my landlord, even the local weed connection.

And then we decided to play. We set up all the amps and mikes and guitars in Gary's place, cords stretched all over the place. Bellowing forth from the second-floor apartments over Thompson Street, our voices raging in the night air of the Village, Circus Maximus.

"Crazy, all night long," Bruno growled to Pete between songs, as they traded guitars and Pete picked up the lead.

Pete was way loaded, we were all loaded. And Pete was way out of tune, too.

"Pete. Hey Pete," I yelled over the blaring riff, "You can't play that damn thing."

Bruno, the mad maestro, was in my face. "You know what? *You* can't play." And

Bruno started giving me a bunch of stuff, defending Pete. Pete, wobbling in the background.

Everybody else standing around silent and slack-jawed.

And I was gone.

Down the stairs, hand around the neck of my guitar. A guitar, incidentally, which was still plugged in. Which brought the amplifier thumping down the stairs not far behind me, which brought everything *around* the amplifier crashing to the floor.

Craaash. Those amplifiers were perfect instruments of their own demise, the event thundering along Thompson Street at maximum volume.

"It's one of their great bouts," Janet admired. "Even the cockroaches came out and said 'What's going on out there?'"

After a few minutes of screaming at each other in the street, we realized what had just happened. Bob and I walked back into the whispering apartment, snarled in cymbals and guitar cords. We told the room that Circus Maximus was dead.

Our second album would be released within weeks, but the group was finished.

Bob Bruno continues to play jazz in the Washington area and dabbles in experimental comedy.

Gary White is a songwriter whose "Long, Long Time" was a major hit for Linda Ronstadt. Gary lives in Pasadena, California, where he markets replica trains. And he's one of my best friends.

Dave Scherstrom worked a few more weeks as a rock drummer for another band, then never again played professionally. He lives in Northern Virginia and works for the local phone company.

Pete Troutner is out there somewhere.

*   *   *

While all that intrigue was happening, and with the attention that was being drawn by "Mr. Bojangles," David Bromberg and I started getting some gigs together in the Village. Those nights were kinder, calmer, not lost inside loudness and discord. I was in places like the Bitter End, playing my poetry to a small club. Intent faces in the audience.

This felt better. Solo, or duo with David, this was my music. The Bitter End, Gerde's Folk City, the Gaslight were all intimate warm venues where I could see the faces of people. Not some huge flashing room with pot smoke and throbbing strobe lights. I was playing for real people, close enough to talk with between songs. Faces close, wrinkle-smiles, grins and stares. The joy and melancholy of my songs washed over longhairs, blue-hairs, city types, pretty girls, college kids. The lonely and the loved. Close enough to touch.

There was a connection.

Hell, I was happy. People want someone to lift them up, not just come out there and sing sad "somebody done me wrong" songs. I felt I could make them feel better about their lives by letting them share mine. The grin, the song, the music.

The airplay of "Mr. Bojangles" on WBAI had drawn attention, and I was making the first real money of my career. We had all come to New York making five bucks a night and that didn't get a hell of a lot better even when Circus Maximus was rolling. But now clubs were bringing me in; I was Jerry Jeff Walker, singer-songwriter who had brought

"Mr. Bojangles" to town. And overnight, I went from a few bucks a gig to five hundred, six hundred, a thousand dollars a night. I was buying drinks at the Kettle of Fish.

Meanwhile, down in Austin, the first released recording of "Mr. Bojangles" was on the street. Cut by Allen Damron, a 45-rpm single with "Little Bird" on the other side. Allen had recorded my songs and pressed about 1,000 copies as giveaway items when the Chequered Flag opened up.

To get my voice and song on the streets, Dan Elliot, who was still managing me, arranged to cut a demo at Vanguard Records. We cut an acoustic version, Bromberg playing that magnificent guitar, and Bojangles danced alive in David's magic lines.

Vanguard didn't want it. The president of Vanguard, Maynard Solomon, a brilliant man with sterling musical tastes, didn't want it. This was 1968. Martin Luther King Jr. had just been murdered in Memphis, and Solomon found the song a little bit racist.

And remember, "Mr. Bojangles" is about a *white* guy.

Since my own record company didn't want to let me record it for them, we cooked up some kind of deal where they'd let me record it for somebody else but I would still owe them an album somewhere down the road. We said fine and got the hell out of there as quick as we could.

We took it around to other labels, and ran headlong into the other end of the sensitivity spectrum. One corpulent record exec, cigar welded to his lip, kinda peered around his feet on the desk and told me he wasn't gonna cut "no six-minute record about an old nigger and a dead dog."

While all this was going on, a local guy named Bobby Cole heard "Mr. Bojangles" on WBAI and figured it had been released to the market, which it hadn't been. So he cut his version of the song for Date Records, a Columbia subsidiary. Some DJs got his version and started playing it. We got that stopped right away. A songwriter may not have many rights, but there is the right to choose who records the song the first time. I wanted it to be me.

Atlantic Records was wild about the song. They wanted it. But then came the agents and the lawyers. I had split up with Dan Elliot, but somehow he retained the publishing rights to "Mr. Bojangles" and a bunch of my earlier songs. It was unpleasant. Lawyers. Lots of people calling each other sonofabitch under their breath. When the dust-up ended, we hooked up with Atlantic's ATCO division and headed for the studio to cut my song.

They flew us down to Memphis and cut the song at American Studios, the home of Sun Records, using the same machine Elvis had cut all his early hits on.

They had arranged for session people to play backup and thought they would get it without David. Bromberg was there in the control room, listening in horror and close to tears as someone else tried to create the magic.

I told 'em, "David's part is what makes it dance."

Finally they decided to put Bromberg in to play his part on twelve-string. That was what the song needed.

David And Me

Come on in, sit down my friend,
it's good to see you again

Put your feet up, there's wine in the cup
and old fences to mend
I haven't seen your smile for quite a while,
so just unwind
Relax your mind and let the time go by.

How is your lady, is she still just as crazy,
what the hell was her name?
Remember the night we all got so tight
we never did catch our plane.
We played guitar all night
in that terminal and had a ball,
we played 'em all, and let the time go by.

You still live upstairs, your cats are all there,
with a dozen guitars?
They say we all change, but I feel the same,
and I know that you are.
They always said we played 'em much too long,
but what's a song, it carries on,
and makes the time go by.

Now I live in the west, of Texas I guess,
old Austin's the best
I'm building a house some miles to the south,
the old bird's gonna nest
And the radio will play our song sometimes
and make me smile, erase the miles
And make the time go by.

*   *   *

We hurried out of Memphis and flew back to New York, to get the single out for Atlantic. Columbia was poised with Bobby Cole's version of "Mr. Bojangles." Virtually the day mine was released, Cole's was allowed to be played. So here were DJs and playlists all over New York, all over the country, with two versions of "Mr. Bojangles."

Both became minor hits, but they diluted each other. If there had only been one recording, it might have soared to the top.

Fortunately, other artists would want to record it as well. It wouldn't go away.

The New York Times printed my picture inside an article bannered "Singer-Songwriters are Making a Comeback. Developing Trend Indicated at the Bitter End by Jerry Jeff Walker and Joni Mitchell."

He veers toward a hip-country style, folkish modern Nashville in a manner that recalls Woody Guthrie, Bob Dylan, Roger Miller and any other rural rambler-bumbler with a funny

hat, a beat-up guitar and a head full of lyrics. At 26, Mr. Walker is sitting on a potential hit recording, his own "Mr. Bojangles."
The New York Times
July 5, 1968

Summer '68 was heady. In late July, I played the Newport Folk Festival. The four of us, David Bromberg, Gary White, Don Brooks and me, all on the same summer stage. The folk festival ran through the weekend, and Monday we were back in New York City for ATCO again.

Holding forth at the Newport Folk Festival in 1968 with David Bromberg (guitar), Donny Brooks (harmonica) and Gary White (bass).

We were cutting tracks for my first solo album, also titled *Mr.Bojangles*. And it was like bringing all those friends from New Orleans and Texas right along with me. The album had "Gypsy Songman" from those French Quarter streets, "Mr. Bojangles" from the First Precinct jail. "Little Bird" from Dallas. And a song I'd written about a whole lifetime in one night, "My Old Man."

My Old Man

My old man had a rounder's soul
He'd hear an old freight train and then he'd have to go
Said he'd been blessed with a gypsy bone
And that's the reason he'd been cursed to roam
Came back through town back before the war
He didn't even know what it was that he was lookin' for
Carried a tattered bag for his violin

Full of lots of songs of the places that he had been
He talked real easy had a smilin' way
he could pass along to you while his fiddle played.

Just makin' people drop their cares and woes
To hum out loud the tunes that his fiddle bowed
Till the people there began to join that sound
And everyone in town was laughin' singin' dancin' round
Like the fiddlers' tunes were all they heard that night
As if some dream had said all this world is right.

His eye caught one dancin' lady there
She had that rollin' flowin' danglin' kind of hair
He played for her as if she danced alone
Played his favorite songs, the ones he called his own
Till she alone was dancin' in the room
The only thing left movin' to his fiddle tune

Played until she was the last to go
Then he stopped and packed his case, said he'd take her home
And all the nights that passed, a child was born
And all the years that passed, love would keep them warm
And all their lives they'd share the dream come true
All because she danced so well to his fiddle tunes

But the train next mornin' she blew a lonesome sound
As if she sang the blues of what she took from town
And all that I recall was what she said when I was young
No one else could really sing the songs he sung.

Yeah, it was another love song. Not really about my dad, Mel. Parts of it were about Grandpa Clyde, parts of it about Mel's dad. Parts of it about me.

A love song doesn't have to be a boy-loves-girl story. Or the hard Nashville "she done me wrong, I got my gun and drove off in m'pickup" song. A love song is about love.

"Mr. Bojangles" is a love song. "My Old Man" is, too.

Deceptively simple in approach, 'down home' in the same sense as his folk forebears such as Woody Guthrie, Walker nevertheless creates a quality of newness in the idiom that should give label-conscious spokesmen a hard time discovering a ready slot to pitch him in.
Variety
August 21, 1968

His singing of his Atco single, 'Mr. Bojangles,' was an example of Walker's performing style. His guitar introduction drew the expected applause from the audience.
He then started to sing another song. The false start even cracked Bromberg up.

Billboard
September 7, 1968

At the Bitter End one night, Harry Belafonte came in, intently listening to "Mr. Bojangles," which he wanted to record and eventually did. And when I played "My Old Man," he sat by the soundboard and he cried.

Lots of artists, by now, were singing my song. But like Ramblin' Jack Elliot, some folks thought the lyrics were so complex they could hardly make it through without a mistake.

"Laughed, slapped . . . how's that line go, Jerry?"

"He laugh-slapped his leg a step."

"Jerry Jeff, this is too cumbersome. We gotta smooth this up."

"Don't you *touch* my song."

"Yessir."

We picked up another roommate one day. A kid named Keith Sykes knocked on the door, said he had just hitchhiked to New York, and he loved "Mr. Bojangles." He was writing songs, and now he was sleeping on the floor just like we'd all done, just like the next crop would. Janet and I had another boarder. And down the road, I would wind up cutting a few of baby Keith's songs.

There was a problem with all this success and all the hefty checks made out to Jerry Jeff Walker. My legal name was still Ronald Clyde Crosby. Cashing those checks was a hassle. So Janet and I got a lawyer, whole thing cost about thirty-five bucks. And we had our names changed. Now, I was legally Jerry Jeff Walker.

Janet would get off work, come home and cook supper for all of us before we had to hit the clubs for our gigs. We'd play a set and roll back into the apartment.

Our lives were full of feelings of friendship, warm as the first skin blush from sipping red jug wine. We walked the streets, sat on wooden floors, made music with good true friends. David and Gary. Keith Sykes. Donny Brooks. That special sensitive artist, Paul Seibel, the brilliant songwriter, a man with a shy and perfect heart.

Townes Van Zandt would glide into town every now and then, an old buddy from the Houston couch days. He was playing some New York clubs and would drop by our place to talk. Janet said he reminded her of an Indian ghost. Tan, tall, thin, leathered. Speaking seldom, with the softest of whispers.

Ben Jennings, on his merriment circuit, would spend about four months in New Orleans, four months in San Francisco, then show up in New York, towering in some doorway, bellowing hello. This year's door-knock found Ben's endless arm around Luwanda, whose great-aunt's passing had left her with $5,000.

Ben had always wanted to see Paris.

Luwanda, Ben, and the magnificent poet Charles John Quarto came to our place for the evening. After drinking pretty steadily all evening, we decided we really needed to see Quarto's friend play saxophone at a gig in Hoboken. The last train had left. We tried to find the place through a succession of cabs whose drivers seemed distracted by a taxi full of slobbering drunks. We never found the place and finally decided to go home.

So, dammit, if I couldn't go to Hoboken, I was gonna do the next best thing. I'd go to Paris with Ben.

I groaned into the phone to my manager.

"Yep, we wanna go to Paris . . . Tonight . . . Yep . . . Nope, we don't have reservations . . . Nope, I don't have a passport . . . Nope, no money . . . Yep. OK."

That passport. I'd been looking for a passport since my days as a street singer in New Orleans, dreaming of shipping out with the Merchant Marine, but carrying the identification of a man named Jerry Ferris.

We got to Paris, rented a car. I terrified the rest of them by driving, terrified all except Ben who demanded that I continue with my experimental left-side-of-the-road steering. We ended up going around the Arc de Triomphe about thirty times before we got over to the funky side of Paris.

We found this hotel, almost a rooming house. A couple of floors up, little balcony overlooking the streets and cobblestones, and Paris worked its magic. Janet, Ben, Luwanda and me. Rain-wet stone streets, all the mist and mystery. About thirteen bottles of champagne later, we were all drunk.

We wandered along the street in a soggy night. At one point, Ben was going to jump into the Seine and commit suicide. Soon each of us made the same pledge.

"This is it," Ben grinned. "This is what the poet should do. Jump into the Seine and drown." He nodded at us with impish invitation.

There, under a bridge on the Seine, we came upon an old wino, resting on a bench. He got up and walked toward us. I shoved that last bottle of champagne in his hands.

"Here, friend. This is yours."

For the third or fourth day, it continued to rain, and I was very melancholy. I went down to the streets with Ben and bought three or four bottles of wine and some cheese.

We sat on our balcony and watched the street sweepers and their brooms. And I pulled out my guitar and played "My Old Man" while Ben stared into the rain.

Janet and I flew home, leaving Ben and Luwanda behind in Paris to work down the rest of that five grand. What we had just lived became a song, "Janet Says."

Janet Says

Janet says it looks like a rainy day today
Just another rainy day
As I lean my chin slowly up against the window pane
It's another gray rainy day
But go on try it again
Try, try, try–try to get goin'

But the rain comes down
Forcin' you to stay inside
Holdin' you back from
The places that you usually hide

Are you all alone? Or more than anything before?
Janet says she loves you,
Is there something troublin' you?
It's not that easy to say
For I feel at times such a presence

In the room of friends I knew
Especially on these rainy days
But go on, try to stay
Fly, fly, fly, we're flyin' away

We hold on to memories of everyone
Like existing clouds — a shadow dance before the sun
And down with the rain
I can see the separations come

Janet says maybe you would rather sing to me
It might be easier that way
I guess it would, and it ought to be a simple melody
One that sort of suits the rain
Everything rolls off unwinding reels
Of remembering how it used to feel
To belong to someone

Life was moving fast. After so many years of hitchhiking and nights spent on the streets or on borrowed couches, my existence had become a warm Manhattan apartment, a vintage Corvette in an expensive parking garage, whiskey and music all night, enough money and enough fame to keep it going endlessly. Day after day, into the nights which became morning.

A scene from that life, shortly after we returned from Paris: me, Janet, an acquaintance named Michael.

"What's Jerry doing?" Michael asked.

"He's going to take some money and he's going to leave town," Janet said.

"Aren't you gonna stop him?"

"Why would I want to do that?"

"I'm going across the street and I'm gonna get some wine," I told them.

"Are you really gonna get wine?" Michael asked.

"Yeah. He's gonna get wine," Janet said.

I came back about three days later.

Sometime the next day, Michael looked at Janet and said, "I don't understand all of this."

"Good. You're one of us."

A sadness had surfaced. Some of it worked its way out positively in my songs, in the music offered to those softly lighted faces each night. Some of it lay imbedded, and it bought me another round.

The drinking was never really a problem then, at least it didn't seem to be a problem. But for those whose lives I most directly touched, the bottle was less than a friend.

In my mind I was asking, "Who's in charge here?" I played acoustic music, nobody wanted it. I played electric music and everybody got excited but, shit, my acoustic music passed me by. Janet was great because she let me follow my head, which was kind of like, "I need to keep pushin' this thing to see what else happens."

There was also life going on out there, and I wanted to experience it. I was working a lot and making lots of records. I wondered why, of all my talented friends, I was picked to stand out.

I still owed Vanguard an album, which became *Driftin' Way of Life*, in 1969. The songs were about my life. The title song itself told a lot. My love song to Sally Ann Mitchell was on there too, "Morning Song to Sally." And there was "Ramblin' Scramblin'."

The album had a real strong country feel. There was no question that in 1969 my music had taken a definite turn, and it was an extremely comfortable sound for me. I felt like I was headed home.

The jacket photos on *Driftin' Way of Life* had been taken while we were still living on Thompson Street. I just stepped outside our place and climbed the roof and fire escapes while the photographer clicked away. And we did the same thing inside, trying to wedge me and the photographer into the same corners of that little empty apartment. I sat on our dresser for one picture. It was about the only piece of furniture we had. Probably Armando the janitor's rummaging handiwork.

In March of 1969, I was back in the studio for ATCO, cutting tracks for *Five Years Gone*. This had some of my newer work on it, including "Janet Says" from our lunatic Paris trip, a Michael Murphey tune, and a song by our old Thompson Street buddy, Keith Sykes. So by the end of the year, I had two albums out on two different labels.

Then spring came with its beautiful sky. Except I couldn't see it. I tried to strain my head to see the sky but couldn't for the buildings in the way.

It was time to leave.

Janet agreed. She said, "Look, you came to New York. You've paid your dues. You made contacts, maybe it's time to go."

So we looked in the paper and found a used 'Vette for sale upstate. We took a train up and bought it. Put our stuff in storage and headed out to America with the top down.

We had been in New York too long. And it still didn't feel like home. Back in Texas, they always thought of me as one of them. So Janet and I drove to Austin in our little red Corvette.

Austin in 1969 was still that small college town, but it was stirring, it was cooking, something was happening there. I played the Chequered Flag's July Fourth "American Folk Festival," which drew about 6,000 people. Heady stuff. By mid-October, I was headlining a show at the Municipal Auditorium, with Gordon Lightfoot and Jimmy Driftwood.

But after being trapped in New York for such a long and volatile period, I wanted to keep moving.

Pisces always return to the sea. I felt that maybe Florida and the Keys might hold the answer to all I longed for.

We got in the 'Vette and headed once again through Louisiana, past New Orleans on down to the Keys.

I owed Atlantic Records another album. So they thought maybe Criterion Studios in Miami might work. The Bee Gees had cut there, and Atlantic was moving its studio band there.

These were the same guys who had cut the "Mr. Bojangles" single. Charlie Freeman, Tommy McClure, Sammy Creason and Jimmy Dickerson made up the group. They called themselves the Dixie Flyers.

I said, "I'll give it a try."

I had more offers to tour because of "Mr. Bojangles," but I could fly from anywhere and play.

Janet and I landed on a little island up from Key West called Summerland Key. I was gone a lot, running up to Miami between gigs, recording that project for ATCO. Janet was going a little stir-crazy with the locals while I was gone. I don't blame Janet, she followed my lead. Also, Janet always liked to work, and the Florida Keys are for people who stop working. They doze off all the time. They play cards and shuffle-board. They fish and get drunk. Watch TV and basically let life pass them by. We were young and we needed to get on with life.

I bought Janet a motorcycle, a BSA 650 Gold Star, to get around on while I was gone. I got visions of riding to gigs. Going through life on a 'cycle. But first I had to make an album, *Bein' Free*, in Miami.

Janet decided she wanted to go to California.

And I could slowly implode in the Keys.

Janet bought a Volkswagen camper bus for a long drive through the Southwest to San Francisco. She lives there still today, designing upscale women's clothing and fragrances. Soon after our breakup, she changed her name to Kat.

"A catwalk is a narrow walkway, a single plank," she tells only a few folks. "Somewhere along the line I just thought I was a catwalker. Kat Walker."

Help Me Now

Hear me now and use your love to listen well,
'Cause I'm tryin' to tell you why I know
It's time for me to go
I drifted into the city to sing
my songs of the gypsy life
Be free, be kind, be strong
I sang at walls,
And you came down to hold my head
When the concrete beat me down
And we rested high in a nest in the wall
Forgetting it all
So help me now, I do believe I'm sinkin' down
Yes, I'm back on the ground and I've found
I'm bound to travel on
You've only asked me to let you know
Whenever I had to go
I'm tryin' to let you know I'll soon be gone
I want it clear and my thoughts in here
So you'll know you're not to blame
It's those cats upstairs who handle my songs
How they string me along
Lovin' someone is to love someone

Forever is the moment you're in
A woman's a world a man can rest inside
It's a love that's sown with dreams
That the city keeps tearin' on down
And can't you see what you're lovin' in me
Is my will to be free
So help me now to understand
I'm a free born man
And I do love you so
But now it's time
For me to go.

Chapter 7

The best way to see Canada . . . 'Mr. Bojangles' is everywhere . . .
The Flying Lady . . . The destiny of Jimmy Buffett . . . Fear and
loathing in Key West . . .

Looking back, I want to say that the three years I spent with Janet were wonderful.

She gave me stability and a sense of place that I'm sure I needed. I had to stick with the band thing. I needed that experience, learning how to work with other musicians to get the most out of my music. Eventually, though, I came to feel that it was a dead-end road.

Playing with studio musicians wasn't working out, either. I needed a band of my own.

I didn't know it fully, but I had a feeling that the music I liked happened because the whole group lived and played together — they had like interests.

I would find my spot somewhere.

I would have to keep moving.

Not long after Janet headed out, my driver's license was suspended. After a fight in a Key West bar, where I had been drastically overserved, I tried to fly the Corvette up the Causeway to Coconut Grove, me behind the wheel with Ben beside me wailing on a mouth harp. I got as far as the entrance to the highway, where the 'Vette swapped ends a couple of times.

The cops pounced on us within seconds.

OK, no driver's license. Wasn't the first time and wouldn't be the last. Somebody told me that a motorcycle license might be a convenient way around that. So during an out-of-town gig in Washington, I applied locally for a motorcycle license and got it without any checks or delays.

I still had the BSA 650 that I had bought for Janet to ride. A few trips up and down U.S. Route One between Key West and Coconut Grove on the bike's rough suspension convinced me that BSA really meant Bloody Sore Ass. So I traded it for a Harley Sportster.

I wanted adventure. My mom and dad had honeymooned on an Indian, so I had motorcycle blood. I told my office to book me across Canada.

I bought the Harley from Ray Carter, a car mechanic who really wanted to be an artist, a sculptor, painter. He'd seen metal sculptures outside airports and public buildings and thought, like the rest of us, "Shit, I can do that." He figured he could sculpt just as well as any of these people who make swans out of car fenders.

Ray and I loaded our motorcycles into the back of a U-Haul trailer, along with some artwork and miscellaneous crap, and drove all the way from the Keys to upstate New York. Ray decided to stay in Woodstock. I visited my folks in Oneonta, took my mom for a ride on the motorcycle.

I bought a poncho and a piece of foam rubber to wrap around my guitar case to ward off rain. The suitcase was strapped to a luggage rack, and it lined up just right with the seat. I nailed a reflector on the end of my guitar case, and stuck it out off the back of the motorcycle. Tied the whole mess down with bungee cords. With the foam rubber padding, I could lean back and have a pretty comfortable backrest for the ride.

This was how I traveled across Canada, hitting the gigs that my booking agent had scheduled.

In Ottawa, I appeared on a local TV talk show. The host was a good-looking Irish redhead — Marianne. After the program, everybody adjourned to a bar.

I said, "Well, I'm riding a motorcycle, so I'm not drinking."

And Marianne said, "Well, I am. And I'm gonna have a big martini."

We got so drunk Marianne had to help me onto the motorcycle. Then she got on behind me. That's when I realized that I probably wasn't going to have much luck with the discipline of not drinking while riding motorcycles.

The cold wind sobered me up, and I got us home. Her home. After a hot shower and some good hash we settled into her cabin for a long night of love.

In Montreal, a few days later, there was Cindy. Beautiful. Legs. "I'm thinking about going to Paris," she said during a break in the action one night. It was an invitation.

I thought, "Shit. I just got this trip going. Do I really want to give up on this and follow this lovely to Europe?"

I almost did. Until one day when I woke in her bed, looked out the window, and found a blue-sky morning. I thought, what a great day it would be to hit the road with my bike.

She saw the look. She kicked my ass out of the house and down the street, and I was gone.

I rode through Canada to Rivière du Loupe, to New Brunswick, hopped boats to Newfoundland and Nova Scotia. Turned back down into New Hampshire and Massachusetts and got back to Woodstock by the fall. There I met some of The Band. Picked with Rick Danko. Hooked up with Fred Neil, a gifted singer-songwriter whose work I much admired (and still do). But the snow flurries were starting and Woodstock winter was coming, so Ray Carter and I loaded up the motorcycles again and headed south with a U-Haul.

I remember this lovely waitress in New York. I was going to take her south. Didn't. Ray talked me out of it.

And that kind of made me sad. So I got pretty drunk in the car, thinking about the girl I didn't go to Paris with and the girl in New York I didn't bring south.

The fall leaves rushed by the windows outside. I just rode along, drinking, drunk, watching the trees blur past, until I fell asleep in the car.

Then, somewhere around Virginia or North Carolina, Ray shook me awake.

"Didn't you tell me you wrote 'Mr. Bojangles'?"

"Yeah, I did," I said, rubbing sleep fog from my eyes.

"I don't know, but for the last two or three hours I've been driving this car, every station on the radio keeps playing a song called 'Mr. Bojangles' by some group called the Dirt Band."

He started punching buttons on the radio, and before he hit three or four of them, we found it again. "*. . . Knew a man, Bojangles and . . .* " It was all over the dial.

I remembered the Nitty Gritty Dirt Band telling me they were going to record the song. But at that time, in the first two years of the song's life, there had been about fifty recordings. Everybody said they would make it their radio-play single. Tom Jones, Harry Belafonte, Lulu. Nobody from the younger groups had done it, though.

Jimmy Ibbotson of the Dirt Band told me how they came to choose it for their record. When Jimmy graduated from college in 1969, he packed his '62 Dodge Dart for the cross-country drive from Indiana to California. One of those life-beginning journeys. While he was loading the trunk, he was approached by a girl his buddies considered "a good witch."

Long hair, dyed black. Paisley muumuu, broad-brimmed straw hat, purple granny glasses. She reached down inside a leather mailbag which she carried across her shoulder, and instead of producing the usual weed or mescaline, she pulled out a 45-rpm single in a brown paper sleeve. It was my recording of "Mr. Bojangles."

"I know this will mean a lot to you," the good witch said, and she walked away.

Ibbotson tossed the 45 in the trunk, finished packing his car, and drove to California.

There, he hooked up with the musicians who would later form the Nitty Gritty Dirt Band. Months later, they were looking for songs for their concept album. Jimmy Ibbotson remembered that record stuck somewhere in his car.

In the parking lot of a Jack in the Box in Los Angeles, Ibbotson begin to dig through the trunk of his Dodge Dart, under the cardboard box filled with stinky T-shirts, under his guitar case, under the spare tire. In a puddle of rusty water in the wheel well, he found the crusted single in the brown paper liner.

They went to somebody's mom's house, where there was a record player. But the hi-fi amplifier was blown. So the guys bent close to the turntable, listening to the faint sounds that emanated from the diamond needle as it scratched along the grooves.

That long-haired huddle over the phonograph produced some bent lyrics. "He spoke right out" became "The smoke ran out." And the line which almost every singer finds challenging, "He laughed-slapped his leg a step," was sung, "He laughed and clicked his heels and stepped."

The Dirt Band got their concept album, complete with tapes of someone's Uncle Charlie playing harmonica with a howling dog, couple of songs from Mike Nesmith, a few from Kenny Loggins, and this five-minute love song written by Jerry Jeff Walker. They blew the doors off with the album and radio play of the album's single, "Mr. Bojangles."

I was partly responsible for the success of an album headlining a barking dog.

With that hit single out there — even though it wasn't my recording — my booking prospects started to improve. I was still playing a duo with Bromberg, but I was looking for a band.

We headed into the studio in Miami with the Dixie Flyers and began to record my album *Bein' Free* for Atlantic. I had met these guys and liked them. Charlie Freeman, Sammy Creason, Tommy McClure, Mike Utley, Jim Dickinson, Bobby Woods. Don Brooks dropped in on harmonica. But they were R&B-ing the music. They had a hard time being country.

I was still searching for a band that was tuned into my idiosyncratic folk-country-rock approach. Where Dylan was already, where Fred Neil had been. Most bands were used to rigid count-offs and tight tracks and professional singers. I wanted a bunch of guys who would let the rough side drag.

And I wanted guys who were like me personally, too. I wanted to be able to talk with my band, hang out with them, get close to them.

You can't walk in and shake hands with six musicians, then sit down to play and bring a lot to the table. I once cut an album with Nashville session ace Charlie McCoy. I liked mood lighting. He wouldn't play in the dark. So I would record and he'd wait till I finished. Then he'd turn on all the lights in the studio and overdub his parts. And he was pure business. Punch the clock and go. It put a tension in the room.

"Oh, you're singing about an old dancer there? I didn't know that! Never did catch the lyrics to that song."

Back in Coconut Grove, I sold the motorcycle and bought a 1948 Packard, the "Flying Lady." I looked up again with an old girlfriend, Teresa Murphy Sadler, a wild Miami child raised in a Catholic school environment. By her late teens, Murphy had discovered both sex and partying, and she embraced them both with great gusto.

Murphy had run with a shady crowd in Miami that included some characters like "Murph the Surf," the jewel thief who became known for the infamous Star of India caper. I think Murphy Sadler had defected to Key West to get some distance from that rough crowd.

She was a big woman, big boned, bawdy barroom laugh, salty sense of humor. She was an ex-stripper, had a baby boy. And she had a lot of no-good friends who were always ready to party.

There was one guy, Rocky, who had done so much cocaine his head would whistle like a flute when he rode his motorcycle. Nose, septum, completely gone. Rocky was the point man. He'd score a couple of pounds and cut it up for the bands. There was a lot of cocaine around, and a lot of people doing it.

I, with the self-discipline of a jellyfish, fell right in with them.

One day, I was driving with Murphy in the Flying Lady through the Grove when we passed this familiar-looking guy riding a bicycle.

"Fromholz!" I yelled.

It was Steve Fromholz from Austin. I backed up, threw his bike in the back seat, and took him home with us. Fromholz was down for a recording session with Stephen Stills at Atlantic Studios. After an evening at our house drinking, talking, laughing, he told us to come with him to the studio for the night's session. The recording started at midnight, everybody working through the night, then dragging out about noon the next day.

As we drove to the studio, Fromholz filled me in: "I'll be lucky to get out of this one alive. There's lots and lots and lots of cocaine here. Bags of blow all around the room. Lots of cocaine madness and egos. Scary. I'm just a country boy. I've been to the big city but not to one this big."

When we tumbled in, about midnight, things were rollin' pretty good.

And right away, in addition to the toot, I sensed the presence of some real assholes. There was an entourage atmosphere. High-dollar rock and roll.

Oh, goody.

I'm a little unclear about the details, but before too long Murphy and I had misbehaved so badly that we not only were tossed out of the studio, but we nearly cost Fromholz his studio gig.

I'm not sure, but I think what got us tossed was Murphy pouring a glass of beer over the head of Stills' manager.

Whatever our sins, Murphy and I hopped in the Flying Lady and headed home.

The old Packard was a terrible car for me to drive. I got drunk too easily and the car weighed about two tons and drove like a tank at the best of times. So it didn't take much for somebody to think you were driving drunk. Especially if you were driving drunk.

Before we got home from the studio, I put the Flying Lady over a curb and bent the front end, and we had to tow her away.

Enter destiny. Not mine, but Jimmy Buffett's.

*   *   *

Buffett was a new friend. We had recently met at a concert in Jackson, Mississippi. A field house on a Saturday afternoon. Nobody came. We just unpacked our guitars at the back of the stage, each taking turns. Jimmy played to me, I played for Jimmy. We packed up to leave.

I said, "Look, I'm heading for New Orleans. Some cold beer and Archie McConnell's corn on the cob."

Jimmy said, "OK if I join you?"

We drove to the Quarter, started walking the streets, making the bars. My kind of guy. Along the way, we bumped into some friends of Jimmy's. Gerry Wood, John Andrews and a guy named Bubba. They told us they were about to leave the next morning on the final run of the "Panama Limited" passenger train from New Orleans to Nashville.

Jimmy said flat out, "We're going."

The train left really early in the morning, which necessitated staying up all night, of course. Jimmy got the sandwiches, I got the beer and booze.

That morning, with the train about to pull out, the five of us were running down the platform. I had a case of beer on my shoulder. A porter hollered, "Welcome aboard, Mr. John. Good to have you."

John Andrews, it turned out, was the biggest train buff in America. He was lead guitarist for the band Mother Earth, traveled to each gig by train, and knew the porters and conductors on every line in the United States.

John saw to it that we were placed in a double Pullman, which opened into one really big compartment. I put the case of beer in the middle of the floor and Jimmy piled some po' boys by the windows. We broke out the guitars and had a party going by the time we rolled out of the yard.

In the course of the day, we absorbed numerous varying reprimands about proper behavior on a train. The conductor took a few nips of our Wild Turkey and spent more time in our compartment than anywhere else.

And on that clattering journey, with the conductor at our side, Jimmy and I started crooning the verses to "Railroad Lady."

Railroad Lady

CHORUS:
> She's a railroad lady, just a little bit shady
> She spent her whole life on the train.
> She's a semi-good looker, but the fast rails they took her.
> She's trying, just trying to get home again.

South Station in Boston to the freight yards of Austin.
Florida sunshine, the New Orleans rain.
Now that the rail packs have taken the best tracks,
She's trying, just trying to get home again.

Once a highballin' loner he thought he would own her
He bought her a fur coat and a big diamond ring.
She hocked them for cold cash, left town on the Wabash,
Not thinking, not thinking of home way back then.

(Repeat chorus)

When we got to Nashville, I spent the night with Jimmy and his wife Margie. We partied some more, then Jimmy and Margie went to bed.

What to do, what to do . . .

I had been out of contact with my Key West friends for a while, so I headed for a phone and began dialing. But the operator said I couldn't make calls, even collect calls, without giving her the number I was calling from. And there was no number on the phone. I made up some long fictitious number which she and I both knew clearly was false.

"No good. I can't put the call through without it."

I tried all kinds of reasoning with her. She insisted she couldn't do it.

"Well, then what will you do about *this*?" I said, and I banged the phone receiver on the table four or five times, teeth gritted.

"Oh?" she said. "Then how about *THIS*!" And she pushed a button that blew a high piercing, screeching wail into my ear.

I quit trying and went to sleep.

The next morning, the phone rings and Jimmy answers. It was the telephone company. His phone service had been suspended. They asked him if he was ready to behave.

Two gracefully aging street musicians meet once again. This is a shot from an episode of
The Texas Connection, **the Nashville Network series for which I was host for two years in the
early '90s.**

He said, "What on earth are you talking about?"

They answered, "Last night somebody at this number gave the operator a hard time."

Jimmy says, "I didn't even use the phone last night."

"Well, somebody at this number did."

Finally Jimmy says, "Wait a minute. I've got a friend staying here who might shed some light on this. In fact, I'm sure that's what happened, and I apologize."

His phone service was restored, and everything was back to normal. He didn't seem to be too upset and handled it well.

After that I figured I owed him some hospitality, so I invited him to stay at my place any time he was in Florida.

A day or two after the Packard got bent, Buffett took me up on the invitation. He got booked for a gig in Miami and flew down to play. When he showed up at the club, they had never heard of him. That old trick. But they gave him a booking about three weeks away. So Buffett was staying with me and Murphy, with nothing to do.

And he was real handy with tools.

We drove out to this place that turned out to be a Packard graveyard. When we drove up, the front yard was full of nautical brass, a lot of great old junk and car parts.

"We're looking for the front end of a '48 Packard."

Some guy waved us past him toward this fenced area. Jimmy and I hopped the fence and looked out upon a sea of about three dozen Packards. We waded through knee-deep grass, walking through the years from the models built before the war, through the postwar era, to the age of rock and roll.

Crawled up inside a few, ants pouring out of the seats in the Florida heat.

We went back inside and Buffett said, "Yep, think you've probably got something out there that'll work."

"Got any tools?" the man asked.

"Well, no, really don't."

He said, "Well, lemme get you some wrenches. And don't lose 'em in the grass." He was a grumpy old guy, but we were young kids, and he must've liked our smiles.

Buffett crawled under a Packard carcass and used borrowed wrenches and jacks to get it loose.

We hauled this front end to a repair garage, Hank and Bill's, where I'd had the Flying Lady towed. Jimmy and I wrote a song about that place. Bill was the one who answered the phone every time it rang. Hank was mainly a pair of feet sticking out from under the car.

Hank and Bill decided to go to lunch, and called Jimmy in to watch the store while they ate. We were now in charge.

Buffett told me, "Man, you sure know how to show a good time in Miami!"

Jimmy was burning out on Nashville. Having grown up in Mobile, he had hot weather and the ocean coursing through his veins. Murphy and I decided to show repairman Buffett some more of our state.

We loaded up the bicycles, tied 'em to the roof, and set off for Key West.

Down the road we went, singing our song about Hank and Bill's.

It's a two-man operation
Ya can't do it by yourself
It's Hank and Bill's
At Porter Road and Twelfth.

Our adventure lasted the entire day. We stopped at every watering hole, beer joint, bait shop and catfish bar between Key Largo and Key West. I had been in most of them before. It was "Hello" at the door, my favorite beer opening as soon as we stepped inside. And soon, they knew Jimmy too.

Finally, we wheeled into Key West and thrust Buffett toward the sand and the ending of the day. We watched his face blush with orange and his blue eyes go sunset.

Buffett filled his lungs, but he wasn't smelling a cheeseburger in paradise. He was inhaling the salt air of his childhood, hearing music in the distance, tasting shrimp in his dreams.

Jimmy had his face in the front door, and the future was saying come on in.

*   *   *

Jimmy Buffett was happy. But I was not, especially. I needed some distance from the wasters in Key West. Summer of 1971, I took Murphy and my trusty Guild guitar out to Santa Fe, New Mexico, and eventually on up to Red River, one of those old mining towns with history and colorful locals. We drew up in a cabin on the Lazy H Ranch, run by a charming character named Harley Bud Johnston and owned by his wife, Judy.

Red River had the Last Run Bar, a joint with a décor of Western memorabilia, critter skins and handicrafts. The folk group Three Faces West was playing there with a young songwriter, Ray Wiley Hubbard. And hanging up over the bar, I found a piece of me. The Angel.

Yeah, the old Roy Smeck Stage Deluxe, the guitar from the French Quarter, emblazoned with Ben Jennings' black ink sketch of an angel. Babe's name, carved in the wood by the drawing. Ray owned that guitar now, those thousands of miles and years away. He let me take the guitar to my cabin one night, where I wrote all night and the next morning about the guitar and my travels with her.

The next evening at the Last Run Bar, I played most of that new song for the crowd, holding back the last verse. That verse hinged on Ray Wiley Hubbard, whether he would trade the old beat-up Angel for my nice big Guild guitar. Everyone wanted to hear that last verse. Ray finally relented.

And that last verse became present tense, "as it travels with me always." That's how songs get written, Gonzo-style.

One afternoon, Harley Bud came by the cabin and hollered, "Come on. I got to get to town. Judy wants me to get forty dollars' worth of dimes for the bar."

So I hopped in the truck, figuring we're coming right back.

We went straight to the Last Run Bar. Harley Bud ordered a beer. His change for a buck, ten cents. He slapped the dime on the bar.

"That's one."

Harley Bud did not enjoy being an errand boy.

During our stay in Red River, Allen Damron passed through with news from Austin. He said that Hondo Crouch had purchased Luckenbach, Texas, which was pretty much nothing more than a few old buildings and a beer joint/post office.

Or post office/beer joint.

He said Hondo could spit and whittle and just be Hondo there in his own town. "You need to see it," he said.

Somewhere, deep in my mind, I must have been thinking about Austin again. The palm trees and waters of Key West seemed so removed from Texas.

I had to figure out how to make this work. I had an office in New York, a record deal in California, my belongings in Key West, and I'm traipsing all over New Mexico with an ex-stripper and a beat-up guitar. And I've just traded in a perfectly good Guild F-50 rosewood which, by the way, the company was preparing to call "The Jerry Jeff Walker" model until I pissed that one away.

With all that bearing down on me, I went back to Key West and fell in with the wasters again. I drank nonstop and plowed a furrow through the cleanest cocaine in south Florida. I started partying day and night, driving back and forth between Key West and Miami with disastrous results.

The Packard, the Flying Lady, was driving herself much of the time. Her lethal metal was heaven's grace away from tragedy. A DWI was trouble enough. It was becoming a habit.

Police report: Finger-to-nose test: completely missed
Clothes: black and white checkered shirt long sleeve Levis dungarees blue looks like they've been worn several days

I crashed on so many couches and stayed up so many nights, I'm not sure where I lived. It turned out the local judge's son was a lawyer. So it was a pretty wise move to hire the son. Give him 500 bucks and it all goes away. I also was getting the word that I ought to take my act somewhere else. They knew I wasn't a smuggler, but they also knew that I was trouble.

One evening Tom McGuane, the novelist, stopped by one of my haunts and said to me, "Man, don't waste your talents like this. We're all getting a bit worried about you. Maybe Key West just doesn't work for you."

Tom had been hard on himself. He had pulled himself out of his own nosedive by suddenly thinking, "One day I'll wake up and look at a bookcase and say, 'I used to do that.'"

I thought after he left, "He's been reading my mail."

On my thirtieth birthday, March 16, 1972, I was roaring my tits off. I wound up on Stock Island, at a bar, with the Angel guitar beside me. The bar was a real smuggler's hangout, full of lowlifes. An old German woman was playing me "Happy Birthday" in German on the jukebox. She was trying her best to cheer me up, but I was sinking.

I kept thinking, "I'm looking for the right combination, a place to play music with a band of musicians who live and love the same things I do. Where you can write something funny or heartfelt, and they'll instinctively know what to play."

I was thrown in with studio musicians who were punching a clock, making albums every four or five months because the contract said I owed 'em one.

I had come to dread the studio. Bright lights, lots of machines. Tape's running — now pick!

The music "business" was driving me crazy. Instead of making me happy, it had brought fights over publishing. The single of "Bojangles" had caused a fight between two record labels, Atlantic and Columbia. Bob Cole's version and my version had gone head to head the whole time it was out.

The record company had added strings on my version without telling me. Then they wouldn't let me record with the pickers I thought might help me. (No mixing Memphis and Nashville studio guys.)

It was no fun.

I had gotten lucky with "Bojangles," but I didn't feel like I was going anywhere unique. In fact, I felt more confused about everything.

Key West was not a music town. It was full of people who specialized in screwing off and were tempting me to do the same. I felt I wanted to quit. Here I was thirty years old, and I wasn't sure this is what I wanted to do.

I had sort of drifted into it. Hell, I hadn't even picked my own name! I had to break loose completely.

And I did, right then, on my birthday night at the bar on Stock Island. I exploded.

I plucked the Angel from my feet, and smashed her once, hard, on the top of the bar. And walked out. Left the pieces there.

Next morning, Ben Jennings was walking the beaches of Stock Island. He saw a child walking along with a tiny fist around a fragment of wood and wire. And Ben saw a shard bearing a drawing of an angel, drifting across the sand.

"Dragging the Angel"

Chapter 8

**Austin goes musical . . . Cosmic cowboys . . . Hondo Crouch . . .
Go beyond it then back up a little bit . . . Magic in Luckenbach . . .
How to spell M-O-T-H-E-R . . .**

I gave the Packard to a friend in Miami, and Murphy and I flew to Houston to get on Texas soil as soon as possible.

I rented a car and drove west. We had been flying in a rainstorm all the way from South Florida to Houston. But as Murphy and I passed Navasota, Texas, the sun came out. Blue skies all the way to Austin. Good omen.

We took an apartment in a complex known as "Outlaw Arms." Pickers and general hangers-on. A loose bunch but friendly. I hit it off with everybody real quick. Grandma Jessie always said, "Your problem is that you're too well liked."

On the way home one night, shortly after we'd arrived in Austin, I stopped at a Seven-Eleven to get some beer. As I was coming out of the store I saw this really ugly mutt of a dog hanging around my car. I hadn't had a dog in years.

I picked him up, got him a can of dog food to eat on the floorboard, and sped homeward. Speed is the operative word here because halfway home a cop pulled me over.

As I got out of the car to show him my driver's license, the dog jumped out and ran into the bushes. I ran after him. The cop called for backup. When I came strolling out of the bushes with the dog, three cop cars surrounded my car.

The cops were all hunkered down behind their cars. I said, "Great of you guys to make such a big deal out of my return to Austin."

They informed me that I was under arrest. They were poking their lights into the car looking everywhere for anything to hang on me.

I explained, "If you're looking for drugs, they're in the spare tire in the trunk."

I knew the car was clean since I'd just rented it a few days ago, but they went bananas ripping the trunk apart.

After we got to the station house they let me make a phone call. I called Murphy to come and bail me out. She came down, took one look at the dog and said, "I don't know any guy who'd have a dog that ugly," and she left me there in jail.

The next day I bailed myself out and went my merry way.

Austin had been a sleepy college town, with the University of Texas adding about 40,000 students to a mix of ranchers, politicians, writers and musicians.

It was the cheapest city of its size in the United States to live in as late as 1975. This made it a great place for artists to live affordably and have a loose lifestyle around them.

T-shirts and jeans and pickup trucks were the trappings of the average Austinite. Because of the college situation the bars were mostly beer and wine. Last call was at 11:30 p.m., bars closed at midnight, and the locals all gathered at each others' houses to party late into the night. Because it didn't cost very much, we could do this night after night and have money left over.

In 1971, the Texas Legislature sinned. Lawmakers changed a long-standing blue law of the Bible Belt and permitted liquor to be sold by the drink. Before that, customers had to brown-bag their own booze into the clubs. There wasn't much money in a club beyond setups and cover charge.

Liquor by the drink meant more profit for club owners. That meant new clubs, new gigs, more music, more musicians. Before long, Austin's sidewalks bobbed with young talented folks, guitars slung over their shoulders, soles worn thin, eager to pick and sing. Struggling bands, which had played for tips and frat parties at the University of Texas, suddenly were in demand.

Long hair and cowboy hats, rockers gobbling acid bumping into freaks bumping into redneck bands. Country fiddlers in backroad honky-tonks, working cowboys playing Bob Wills swing, folkies born in a new age. All living in Austin, smoking plentiful Mexican weed and having a good time.

Not long after I arrived, I got word from some of the pickers that they'd like to join in and find out what I was up to. Every Sunday there was a jam session at a party house called Hill on the Moon. They'd purchase a couple of kegs of beer and charge a buck to get in. It was basically an all-afternoon-into-the-evening party. We all became familiar with each other's music.

If one of the songwriters got a gig and wanted to take someone from Austin with him, chances were he'd already played with two or three of the guys in town. Whoever was free would go with him to his gig.

Steve Fromholz named this bunch of young colts "The Austin Interchangeable Dance Band."

Everybody in town seemed to know everybody else. Groups would break up and re-form almost constantly, oblivious to genre. A band might have a country picker on guitar, a concert violinist, a rock drummer, a folkie as lead singer, and some guy from a one-stoplight town playing pedal steel. Music fusion.

Kenneth Threadgill, the white-maned, round-faced, potbellied patriarch of Austin's north side, presided over a club that looked like an old gas station, which it was. The Saxon Pub was another great small club for solo acts. The Armadillo World Headquarters was opening, and the Hill Country was blessed with crossroads country dance halls.

After a fire at his home in Nashville, Willie Nelson had returned to Texas with a bunch of songs, a guitar case full of fine weed, and not much else. Now he was playing around Austin and talking to producer Jerry Wexler about a concept album that became *Shotgun Willie*.

Steve Fromholz worked between Austin and Colorado with his lively, humorous songs. Doug Sahm was living in town. B.W. Stevenson, the tender poet, was just starting out. Rusty Wier and his Lavender Hill Express were the hot band in town, packing 'em in every night.

Michael Martin Murphey, my old friend from the Rubaiyat in Dallas, was back in Texas and putting together his first album, for A&M Records.

Willie, Murphey and I kept running into each other around clubs in Austin. Crossing paths, watching each other. Back then, Willie had that nylon-string guitar, cowboy hat, stud in his ear. He was backed by Paul English, a drummer who dressed all in black with a cape. No hat. Willie was up there singing "Hello, Walls" with a caped drummer.

And I'm thinking, "Oh, cosmic time. I can handle this." I was ready for some cosmic shit myself.

I learned, finally, that I had a three-album deal with MCA Records. In fact, money had already been paid to my manager, and spent, and MCA wanted a record. I needed a band. I wanted musicians who listened to jazz and blues, some rock and roll, some country, guys with the background to follow me wherever my impulses led.

I was leaning toward a free-wheeling, open approach, the sounds born at some late-night party where everybody's playing and trying new things, and carrying it over to the next day's rehearsal.

This happened constantly in Austin. You'd play all night with different people, trying out new stuff, listening to other peoples' new stuff, new ideas begetting more new ideas. You'd greet the dawn with a guitar in your hand and some new songs or licks in your head. A few hours later, you'd bring the guitar and the new ideas into rehearsal: "Let's do that one we were doing the other night."

But to pull that off, I needed musicians who were immersed in the music the way I was. Living it, day and night. I had met and picked with Rick Danko and other members of The Band in Woodstock. They were living together and playing together. And that affected how they made music.

I liked that. I wasn't interested in nine-to-five musicians who would show up for a gig, play the same songs the same way night after night, then pack up and disappear until next time. I didn't want just backup. I wanted friends I could play with and live with.

I got a call from Gary P. Nunn. He was Michael Murphey's main man, and he kept tabs on everyone else who was picking around Austin.

Gary had grown up near Lubbock in Brownfield, Texas, where the wind always blows and it seems most males pick and sing. He told us his dad had bought him "a set of drums, a gee-tar, and a little Champ amp." Gary P. could play just about every instrument around a country-western band.

Gary had been ready to call it quits and move to Oklahoma to help farm his uncle's place. But Murphey's arrival in Austin changed that. Murphey and Gary P. had rented a complex of houses, cottages and a rehearsal garage off North Lamar. A tidal flow of musicians passed through, and Murphey had put together a band.

Now Gary was inviting me to his garage rehearsal shack to play some of my songs and meet some guys who had begun working behind Murphey.

Taken onstage at the Kerrville Folk Festival in either 1971 or '72, with the original Lost Gonzo Band members — Herb Steiner (steel), Michael McGeary (drums), Gary P. Nunn (keyboards, just off camera) . . . I had just recently relocated to Texas, and singing in Hill Country felt dead-solid perfect.

Lead guitar was Craig Hillis. Bushy hair, straw hat, big buckle. Played the bands around the University of Texas while he went to school. In the late '60s Craig had been swept into the music fusion down at the Chequered Flag, working in a backup band for Steve Fromholz and Dan McCrimmon.

Playing bass was Bob Livingston, who I knew from California and from Red River during the summer of Harley Bud. Tall, with glasses, professorial, red-sandy hair and beard everywhere — "Cosmic Bob" they'd already nicknamed him. He was part of the Lubbock contingent which had swept down into Austin.

Oh, and happy, horny Michael McGeary, the drummer. Craig Hillis says all drummers have hormone problems. Something to do with tight jeans and sitting down all the time.

Gary P., Hillis, Livingston and McGeary had a deal to play with Murphey when he had gigs. The rest of the time they were free to do what they wanted.

So I started falling by and we played some. Murphey had a preconceived idea of how he wanted his music to sound. But I wanted them to play whatever they felt was right for each song, let it go where it felt best.

One of the first songs I ran down for the band was a tune I'd written about a bootmaker in Austin, Charlie Dunn.

I had always wanted handmade boots, and I went to Capitol Saddlery and met Buck Steiner and Charlie. The thing that struck me was how grumpy and bitchy Buck was and how charming and interesting Charlie was.

I tried to capture the interplay between the two in a song.

Studs Terkel years later would tell me, "The best example of labor and management in a song ever."

The band loved our working arrangement because they were always busy. Murphey and I loved it because they were becoming the best band in Austin. Eventually, I inherited the band when Murphey pulled up stakes and moved to New Mexico.

During the week, if I wasn't on the road, I played the bars in Austin and rehearsed with one group or another. On weekends, though, I began heading out of town, into the Hill Country west of Austin.

In 1966, during one of my early trips through Austin, I had met Hondo Crouch, a Hill Country legend. He owned a 55,000-acre goat ranch near Fredericksburg and was partners with University of Texas football coach Darrell Royal in a summer camp for kids, called Camp Champion, near Marble Falls.

Hondo, John Russell Crouch. Whittled wooden crosses and spoons from twigs he found on the ground, chewed tobacco which he spit into empty brown Pearl beer bottles. He drove a beat-up, slightly leaning pickup truck and dressed like a poor man's Will Rogers. Fiercely sang Mexican folk songs and told Indian tales around the campfires of the Hill Country. He'd been an All-America swimmer at the University of Texas in his younger days. His hometown of Hondo, Texas (hence his nickname) had no lakes or rivers nearby. He claimed to have learned to swim in big puddles of water after rain storms, and twinkled when someone believed him.

Hondo was childlike and gregarious. His wife, Shatzie, restored antiques. They shared a wonderful old stone farmhouse eight miles south of Fredericksburg.

Hondo's gentle nature appealed to me the first time I met him, in '66. And he must've seen something in me, because we hit it off right away.

In '71, Hondo bought Luckenbach, Texas, a neglected old Hill Country town. He wanted a place to drink beer and pitch washers, a place to "be Hondo." And he wanted to revive this boarded-up native treasure. Luckenbach consisted mainly of the post office, which was inside the general store — beer sold down at one end, stamps at the other — plus the dance hall and a few other sun-faded buildings.

When I got back to Texas in '71, I immediately sought out Hondo to see what was going on with him and Luckenbach. That trip west became a weekly ritual. I would work and play hard, then kick back with Hondo and the locals down Fredericksburg way.

I would play songs around the potbellied stove in Luckenbach, and Hondo would sing something in Spanish or maybe do a poem from one of the columns he wrote for the Fredericksburg newspaper under the byline "Peter Cedarstacker." We'd drink longnecks and tell stories all night long, usually winding up at the old Hill Country ranch house to watch the sun come up. It was new and fresh for me, and I was coming alive in this environment. Hearing all this Hill Country history mixed with Hondo's mischief was rejuvenating.

I had the feeling I had come home after all this time. Some pickers to play with, no pressure on the record deal, and the Hill Country to relax me.

I was playing the music I wanted, getting a sound I liked, in a place I wanted to be. I felt so good about things that I even bought a house in the town of Oak Hill, part of south Austin. For the first time since I had hitchhiked out of Oneonta, I was putting down roots, in my own restless way.

*   *   *

In this setting, I began to put together *Jerry Jeff Walker*, my first album for MCA. Naturally, it was created without a definite plan, trusting in chance and chaos.

I have the habit of hearing a song at a party or during a "guitar pull," as some of these get-togethers are called. Then I let it run around in my head for awhile. Later I may call somebody back and say, "That song sticks in my mind. Send me a copy of it, or sing it again over the phone."

A couple of those songs had traveled with me to Texas. I'd made a trip to Nashville to see if I might want to record there, and had looked up Guy Clark, who had moved there from California and had started writing. One of the first things he'd come up with was "Old Time Feelin'," a mood thing, kind of haunting.

He'd also written one about leaving L.A. He called it "Pack Up All Your Dishes," but the chorus was, "If I can just get off that L.A. freeway without getting killed or caught."

One of the first songs I wrote during this period was "Hill Country Rain." People from other places — New York, Nashville, Key West, Miami — all wanted to know, "why Austin?" "Why Texas?" I felt I would just sing an answer: "It's something that I can't explain, like dancing naked in the high Hill Country rain."

The pieces were coming together for an album. I thought I would push it all the way, record it in Austin so that it would have its own feel.

Hondo Crouch was the guiding spirit of Luckenbach. His business card read "Imagineer," and he lived up to that billing. This picture dates from the Luckenbach sessions that made up part of my tribute album to Hondo, *A Man Must Carry On.*

I wanted to preserve the energy and the spontaneity of the rehearsal sessions in Gary P.'s garage. Too often that gets lost when a local band goes out of town to record in a big-time studio. A band may sound great in its own environment; then a record company will fly them to New York or L.A., put them in hotels, let them run up big tabs. They become disoriented and homesick, and they lose the feel of what they're about.

Even if you never leave your home turf, studios will kill creativity. You take a band that seems loose and feels good, bring them into the studio, isolate them from each other in booths. The light goes on, and some guy says, "Play!"

Then everybody becomes self-conscious. They stop the recording and say, "Is

117

everybody really in tune?" Pretty soon you've got an argument on your hands and the mood is gone and everything has gone sideways because of the technical problems.

Or they tell you they've run out of tape or they're getting too hot a reading, or blah-blah-blah, and it starts again and it stops again.

Once you've learned a song, you will never play it five times in a row anywhere but in a studio. After playing it five times in a row you know why. It stops being fun, especially when no one is really sure what's wrong with the first four.

Bob Livingston reminded me that he and the other guys in this new group had never been to a studio to cut a record. But that didn't matter to me. I didn't want experience. I didn't want control. If I had my way, the musicians would be lost in the music, not distracted by the recording process.

I wanted energy. I wanted fun. I wanted spontaneity. Spike Jones meets Eddie Cochran. If I found a place relaxed enough, then maybe we would make some magic.

I'd heard about a place on Sixth Street called Pecan Street Studio. The old building still had the sign outside from the previous business, Rapp Cleaners.

The studio was being dismantled, moving to another location. The control board was already gone. All that was left in the huge empty building was one Ampex 16-track machine sitting on the floor, wires running into it, in a room with metal folding chairs pulled into a ragged circle. Raw insulation flapped off the walls. Burlap was tacked up everywhere to buffer the sound.

Without a board, whatever was played into a microphone would go straight onto tape. Good, I thought, now we'll see what this is all about. If the guitar player gets his tone, and the drummer tunes his heads, and the bass player has his sound, they are all just voices. Put mikes in front of them and turn on the machine. If we aren't pegging meters, we're cool.

This was completely opposite from what everybody else was doing, in booths and isolation. Overdubs had become popular, dubbing again and again. By the time the engineers were finished with the song, it was perfect, but it also had no feel.

There is a lot of perfect music in the world; it's in shopping malls everywhere. You don't hear any of our music in shopping malls.

We must have done something right. You can't shop to our music, but you sure can have fun!

We set up in the big empty studio, all in one room, live. We had a big jug of wine and some beer iced down in buckets. It was like a big party.

We started playing 'em. "Charlie Dunn" and "Hill Country Rain" and "Little Bird." I picked up Guy's song, "Old Time Feeling." I had a little thing called "Hairy-Assed Hillbillies," about meeting Billy Swan and Donnie Fritts out in L.A. "Curly And Lil" was something I'd written about a couple that played in a bar in Key West, a family band. "That Old Beat-Up Guitar," about the Angel. "Moon Child," which I had written after going to see the movie *Black Orpheus.*

We might say something to get us in the mood, get a clean start, then pick. We played a little of everything, one after another, looking for a feel. I kept thinking of early music, Buddy Holly and Chuck Berry, primitive stuff but good vibes, ragged but right.

Austin was so laid back in '72 that we could leave the studio door open to Sixth

Street. The bars closed at midnight. Musicians who were interested in how we were recording would stop in to listen.

As people dropped by, we might ask them to join us. I used two bands, and the album notes for *Jerry Jeff Walker* credit twenty musicians. One piano track is credited to the late barrelhouse piano player, Roosevelt "Grey Ghost" Williams. A friend of his had heard about the sessions and brought him over, and he sat down and played.

I left in a lot of intros. At the beginning of "Hill Country Rain" you can hear Bob Livingston do a gospel call. We were looking for a way to get into the song, and I said, "Do one of your gospel intros." And you hear Bob say, "That intro?"

And he sings: "I got a feeeeelin' . . . "

That's how we got the mood. I didn't care where the energy came from as long as everything was loose and we just had fun. It was under the flag of "ragged but right" — that was our working model.

As a musician, I wasn't really skilled enough to be taking this approach, but I was following my gut feeling. I knew there were simple reasons why people liked some kinds of music. I believed that a good song, done with feeling, counted for something. If the intent was right, the feeling would get across.

I knew the rough side would show, but I thought we were going to get smiles and energy and this feeling of camaraderie and happiness. I probably took it too far, but you never know how far is too far till you get there. We used to say, "You have to go beyond it and then back up a little bit."

To finish the mixes, I rode the Texas Chief to Chicago and the Broadway Limited to New York. Michael Brovsky, the album producer, realized how ragged some of the cuts were. He found a bunch of guys around Kingston, New York, led by pedal steel player Patterson Barrett and pianist Jeff Dufine. Brovsky thought it would be fun to see if I could pick with some of them and take some of the roughest stuff and strengthen it a bit. So I went up to their house and told them how I was approaching this. They liked the idea of what we were trying to do, and they helped me do it.

Michael Murphey had taken the band to New York to play the Bitter End. I went to see the show, got up and jammed with them a little bit, and I said to Murphey, "Hey, tomorrow I got some studio time, why don't you come down and sing and be on 'Old Beat-Up Guitar' to help tie it all together?" And he did. I had written "David And Me" for David Bromberg, so we got David to come by and pick. That's how that whole album fell together.

Kind of scattered, hither and yon.

But I'd like to think that it worked. At times, I know it worked.

*   *   *

One day during my New York trip to mix *Jerry Jeff Walker*, I was walking past Town Hall, an old concert hall in Manhattan, when I saw a big truck with two wheels pulled up on the sidewalk. Big cables ran from the truck into a bathroom window of the building.

A sign on the side of truck read "Dale Ashby and Father Sound Recorders."

I knocked on the door. Dale Ashby opened it, and I asked, "Are you recording something?"

A little gospel music, maestro — onstage at McFarland Auditorium at SMU in Dallas in 1975, winging our way through "Will There Be Any In Heaven": John Inmon, Gary P. Nunn, Donnie Dolan, Bob Livingston, Brother Walker.

He said, "Yes, we're doing a symphony date here tonight."

"Could you drive this studio to Texas?"

Dale said, "Sure."

"Luckenbach, Texas?"

"Give us a map. If it's on the map, we'll get there."

Within days, I was tossing Dale's business card across the desk in the office of my manager, Michael Brovsky. I told Brovsky I was going to do the next album in Luckenbach.

"Oh," I said, "and there's no electricity in Luckenbach. Well, there's electricity, but when you open the beer cooler, all the lights flicker."

I felt that something good always came out of my trips to Luckenbach. I also thought if we could find a way to record something there, we'd have a good time, and the good time would show up on the tape. And we would always have the memory of working there.

We had added Kelly Dunn on organ, John Inmon had come on board to play lead guitar and sing some needed high harmonies, and Donny Dolan had taken over on drums, simple and steady.

The Lost Gonzo Band was rounding into shape, although for a while we used a new name that we picked up by accident, in a moment of happy confusion — true Gonzo fashion. This happened during our first gig in New York, when a reviewer in

The New York Times wrote, "Mr. Walker performed last night with an adept cowboy band."

The next night, I turned to somebody on stage and said, "Hey, did you see *The New York Times*? They say we're an adept cowboy band."

Right away, someone from the audience yells, "What the fuck is a deaf cowboy band?"

That was too good to let pass. We became the Deaf Cowboy Band. We had a drumhead painted showing an old geezer with an ear horn, and we used that name on our next album.

That one came together in a hurry.

I had told Dale Ashby and his father to bring their mobile studio to Luckenbach. Sooner than I expected them, they were parked out on the edge of town, down by Grapetown Creek — "edge of town" being just a sorry rock throw from the little post office. Dale had pitched a tent and was starting to peer gingerly into the beer cooler.

They were ready to record an album. Great. The problem was, I didn't have anything written.

I was struggling, trying to figure out what to come up with. I had the start of a song, "Gettin' by on getting by's my stock and trade, livin' it day to day, picking up the pieces wherever they fall . . . " I wasn't sure what the verses would be, but I thought, "This is a 'feel' thing, not a great lyric."

I had a little ditty, "Sangria Wine." It was a recipe for homemade sangria tied into a recipe for a party as you drink the wine. All those ingredients became the song.

I recut "Little Bird" using a condensed version. The original was an early song and it was much too long. I kept all the same words, but told the story shorter. I thought it was better.

I loved Guy Clark's "Desperados Waiting For A Train." I thought it was the most solid song I had heard in a long time, about a kid following his grandpa around, learning at his side how to be a "big man." When the boy is grown enough to do something with him, the old man is dying: "Hang on, Jack, our train's coming, it's our turn. I need ya," but he's gone.

Michael Murphey had a song called "Backsliders Wine." I felt I could sing this and mean it 'cause I had the reputation, which convinced people I was singing the truth.

That was about it. The magic of Luckenbach would have to make the rest come out.

Off to Luckenbach we went, to see what would happen.

The first two days were mostly setup, getting things miked and getting everyone some separation between instruments. We baffled the dance hall with bales of hay to preserve the ambiance. We wanted it to look and sound like we were having a party in the barn.

It was quiet in Luckenbach during a normal week, and we didn't tell anybody we were coming. Some locals stopped by and drank beer and watched us mess around.

We finally got to where things were ready. Dale said through a talk-back box that he was ready in the truck. He blared out, "If you want to roll one, let's see what happens."

I had run through the changes of "Gettin' By" with the band, so I started in.

"Hey, in the truck. It's Scamp Walker time again. Going to try and slide one by you once more."

Gettin' By

Don't matter how you do it,
just do it like you know it,
I've been down this road once or twice before.

CHORUS:
   Just gettin' by on gettin' by's my stock in trade,
   Livin' it day to day
   Pickin' up the pieces wherever they fall.
   Just lettin' it roll
   Lettin' the high times carry the low
   I'm livin' my life easy come, easy go."

Last week I was thinkin'
It's record time again
And I could see Mike makin' those faces
Ah, Mike, don't you worry
Somethin's bound to come out
Besides, I've been down this road once before.

(Chorus)

Income tax is overdue,
And I think she is too.
Been busted and I'll probably get busted some more.
But I'll catch it all later,
Can't let 'em stop me now.
I've been down this road once or twice before.

(Chorus)

We played an instrumental verse and sang the chorus again, then I made up something about "this wasn't a monster track," show biz term for a big, big seller. But the added verse did keep the record from being real short, and "hell, we've been down this road once or twice before."

A real flippant feel, but fun. I changed the opening to "Hi, Buckaroos, Scamp Walker time again" and we cut it. It felt good, and we were off.

We worked on "Sangria Wine" and "Little Bird" and "Backsliders Wine." We spent a whole day on "Desperados Waiting For A Train."

As we played that one, I noticed that Hondo picked up on the lyrics. He heard the message. At that time, most of the music played around central Texas was dance tunes and old country standards. Play-on-words lyrics and cowboy swing. Superficial stuff, nothing that cut deep to the heart of life.

But this was real. Some day, someone was going to sing this over somebody's grave.

Onstage somewhere in the 1970s, smiling in the face of something or other. Steve Stromholz said he could always tell when the crowd was going south on him. "Shoot the leader, Jerry Jeff!" he'd yell. "They're starting to turn on us!"

Hondo stood next to me with his eyes closed, listening to every word. It's the take we used on the record.

I liked the material we had cut so far, and we were making good times. Sitting under the trees by the beer joint/post office every afternoon, first thing we'd do is get out acoustic guitars and swap songs. Things we were working on, things others had written, some old songs we had liked years ago.

One afternoon, Bob Livingston started playing us a verse and chorus of the song Ray Wiley Hubbard was doing in Red River when Bob last saw him. It went: "Up against the wall redneck mother, mother who has raised your son so well."

We rushed into the dance hall, hollering, "Turn on the machine. We've found something fun."

We played it through, and it had humor and a groove. Bob called Ray in New Mexico and demanded more verses. Ray said, "There's only two. I wasn't really thinking it was a good song anyway."

So we did the two verses and decided to add '50s-style "oooooohs" in the background while somebody spelled the word M-O-T-H-E-R. Like "M is for the memories tattooed on my arm." We thought Bob had the best Texas "good ol' boy" accent, so he should spell it.

We decided to call Austin and announce in the newspaper and on a couple of radio shows that we would do a live concert in Luckenbach Saturday night. But we still didn't have all the material we needed for the album.

At Friday's pickin' under the trees, Gary Nunn played us a song about his trip to England with Michael Martin Murphey, whose first wife was from England. Murphey had booked a few gigs there during that trip, but mostly the trip was for Murphey and his wife to visit her folks. They left Gary in his hotel room because, being from Texas and Oklahoma, he would have so little in common with her family. He'd probably be bored.

Bored enough to write a song.

A song is good in direct proportion to how bad the place is you're in when you write it. Some writers force themselves into stark situations to have no distractions when they write. Monks in a monastery!

By Saturday, we were ready for the live show and we had versions of the stuff we had already cut. If something extra came out, all the better.

We had announced a one-dollar charge for the show so people would be sure to come, and they did — on Saturday night, 900 of them crammed into the old dance hall that held 375. Hondo had to come to the mike and ask people to get down out of the rafters because the old dance hall might fall down.

We played and people were having a good time. Then we played "Redneck Mother." The place went bananas.

The last song was "London Homesick Blues." Gary had asked me if I wanted to sing the lyrics. I said, "You sing the verses. That way we'll get 'em right, and I'll sing on the chorus. And this way if anyone asks you if you ever made a record, you can play them this one."

Well, we started in, and as soon as we got to the chorus the first time, that crowd understood instantly what it was about. Being far from home. A Texan in another culture. Lonesome and missing home. Man, it hit. They went over the top, screaming all through the song.

I broke a string on the rhythm guitar in the second chorus, so during the last half of the song I was out of tune and I felt we had lost the groove a bit. I got a new string and we announced that we were going to play it again. I told everybody to relax and, if they felt like it, join in on the chorus.

When the album cut opens, Gary is trying to calm himself down from the crowd reaction so he can start the song. He says, "Let me get myself back in that place." He means slowed down, lonesome, but it could also mean "when I was in England."

I used that intro to kick it off. When the song ends, we wait for a second, then we break into another chorus of "I want to go home with the armadillo." That encore actually came after the first take when I'd broken the string and the crowd wouldn't stop clapping, so we played it again. We stuck that onto the second take when we mixed the album.

It was magic, just like I thought it would be.

We had kept Sunday, Monday and Tuesday open just in case we hadn't gotten everything we needed. On Monday the boys all met by the trees, and I said, "I got one song I've never played." It was supposed to be for a movie that never got made, a documentary in which several contemporary songwriters were supposed to contribute a new song of their choice. I had chosen the theme of rolling wheels. How we're rushed to the hospital in an ambulance at birth, then wheels carry us through life, then the hearse carries us to the grave. Racing through life.

I still had memories of my grandfather's death beneath the overturned tractor. I remembered pictures of my dad standing by a jeep in WWII. I rode motorcycles. I made up a brother who drives stock cars to an early grave. "Rollin' Wheels." I played it for the band and they were spellbound. When I finished, Herb Steiner, the steel player, was crying. I looked around and everyone said, "We gotta cut it. Now."

After we finished recording I listened to the playback, and it was just as I had I imagined it. Flowing, breathing, up and down like a tipped-over wagon with a bent wheel spinning lazily in the air.

The band smiled. Then they told me.

They'd thought this was an "off day," that they were only going to listen to tapes of the week's work. So just before they got to Luckenbach that morning, they all gobbled some mescaline. And there they were, some of them grinning at me with scary vacancy, some with tear-streaked faces.

All along, I'd thought, "Gee, these guys are really into this song." They were just stoned.

Speaking of stoned, in honor of old friend Hunter S. Thompson, I nicknamed the band the Lost Gonzos.

I had become a fan of Hunter's writing, and Rosalee Sorrells once told me, "You need to visit my friend Hunter in Woody Creek, Colorado. He loves Wild Turkey, too."

So I did, and we spent a couple of nights roaring our tits off around Aspen and wound up singing in his living room to his peacocks.

My Gonzo running buddy Dr. Hunter S. Thompson came to Austin to give a talk and basically hold court. He called me to help emcee and serve as the voice of moderation. That and the drink Hunter is drinking tell you all you need to know.

I decided that what the band and I were doing musically, he was doing in his books. That night at his house we discussed Gonzo-ism: "Taking an unknown thing to an unknown place for a known purpose."

That was us, except we were also lost.

The album was titled *Viva Terlingua*. The name came from a bumper sticker which Hondo had brought back from the big chili cook-off in Terlingua, Texas. That bumper sticker, on the wall of the dance hall, became our album cover, complete with Hondo's gnarled hand pointing to the sign.

Viva Terlingua quickly sold 50,000 copies in Texas, compared to 60,000 in the entire United States. MCA was ecstatic. Something was happening. Some of the executives flew down to a concert to figure out what we were doing.

There was no secret to the album's success in Texas. It had a homegrown feel. The kids liked it because it talked about Texas. It was played by a bunch of us from the state and it was about our region of the country.

I was slowly convincing the band we could play and have fun, and could capture that fun on records. We might not be making technically great records, but we were expressing a spirit. We were pretty much a ragtag bunch of gypsies going down the road.

That was the beginning of progressive country. Michael Martin Murphey's hit of a few months earlier, "Cosmic Cowboy," had given it an image. Now we were giving it a sound.

Chapter 9

I met a girl in Texas . . . Stirring that Gonzo stew . . . *Viva Terlingua* and sold-out venues everywhere . . . 'You boys sure look like you're havin'fun' . . .

The mid-'70s in Austin were the busiest, the craziest, the most vivid and intense and productive period of my life. Between 1972 and 1978, I cut nine albums. Each year during that period, I played upwards of 200 dates and wrote dozens of songs. At the same time, I was falling in love, becoming a father, creating friendships that persist to this day, and suffering a loss that still grieves me.

Greased by drugs and alcohol, I was also raising the pursuit of wildness and weird-ness to a fine art. I didn't just burn the candle at both ends, I was also finding new ends to light. Somebody somewhere may one day manage to cram more living into a few years, but I doubt it.

My house in Oak Hill became pretty notorious for wild parties.

During one of those parties I was explaining Fred Neil's music to this guy who ran a club. I played Fred's records. The guy could feel they were good, but he couldn't understand why, if it was good, Fred Neil was not well known.

I told him, "It doesn't matter. As long as you find something in it you like, then dig it!"

He asked, "Where does this stuff come from?"

I replied, "There's great shit all around you if you just tune in and look for it."

After thinking a moment I said, "You spend too much time watching TV."

"Yeah," he says. "But how do you break that habit?"

"Easy!" I answered. "Grab the other end of this TV set."

We picked up the TV, walked across the living room and out the sliding glass door to the swimming pool.

Standing on the side of the pool I counted, "One! Two! Three!"

By my own force I twisted the TV out of his hands and into the pool.

"There you go. Now you're free! Just go home and throw your own TV away. Just like that."

He just stood there dumbfounded, staring at the TV bobbing in the pool.

One morning for breakfast we had a nude volleyball tournament in the pool. Theresa Murphy and I started accusing each other of all kinds of stuff, some true, some not, but all plausible. We almost pushed each other to do things in an OK-I'll-show-you kind of way.

Two headstrong people is an all-right situation, but not with drugs and alcohol mixed into it. I finally called it quits, and she returned to Miami.

While I was working on *Walker's Collectibles* I would sometimes carry around the "acetate," which is an album cut in advance of the final that you could play maybe thirty times before it would wear out. I could still call in any changes to the mastering plant. I would take the acetate to friends' houses and parties and play it on different stereos to hear how the mixes sounded.

One night I dropped by a party at a house on Ninth Street, rented by a barmaid named Cookie DeShay and a writer named Jay Milner. The third tenant of the house, whom I hadn't yet met, was a girl named Susan Streit, who worked at the Texas Legislature.

Susan was playing some Rolling Stones albums. She would leave the room to go fix somebody a drink, and I would put on my acetate; I'd listen for awhile, then drift off in conversation. Susan would change the record back to the Rolling Stones again.

Finally, as the party was winding down, we met at the record player. She wanted to know, "Are you the asshole who keeps changing my records?" I sheepishly said I was, because I was listening to a new record I would put out shortly.

"What do you mean? You actually carry *your own* music when you come to a party at someone's house? *That's unbelievable!*"

Susan decided to talk to me in the kitchen while she made some breakfast. I was worn out, she had to go to work, and we made a promise to meet for dinner after work.

We were inseparable from the start, dividing time between her place and mine. A lot of people were crashing at my place, and between the two of us, we ran most of them off for a while.

Susan was from a different world than mine. She had gone to college, majored in government, and had worked for a congressman in Washington, D.C., before she returned to Texas.

She wore dressy clothes and I wore beat-up jeans. She had a sports car; I had a pick-up truck and a Cadillac convertible. She worked days, and I worked nights. She ran with writers and politicians; I hung out with pickers and songwriters.

Actually, in those days, everybody in Austin hung out with everybody else.

One of our mutual friends was Edwin "Bud" Shrake, a writer and reporter for *Sports Illustrated*. He told me that writers used to be the celebrities of Austin until all the musicians showed up. Bud also wrote novels and had a wonderful sense of humor.

Bud and I could drink. And we did. During the mid-'70s we were the last two still standing at the end of most parties. Bud had come to Luckenbach during the recording of *Viva Terlingua*, and a whole group of his friends sat under the trees at a big picnic table. They had dubbed themselves Mad Dog, Inc. — "Doing indefinable services to mankind." Their password was "Where's mine?"

Bud introduced himself to me at a party, and we hit it right off. Serious talk mixed with cosmic bullshit. Throughout the evening he kept calling me Jacky or Jacky Jack. I thought maybe he was drunk or hadn't gotten the name right.

He said, "No, no. Anyone I've ever met in Texas whose name started with a "J" was a John or Jack, but you've got two J's, and neither one is a Jack, so you'll be Jacky Jack."

Novelist, screenwriter and all-star sports journalist Edwin "Bud" Shrake knows where all the bodies are buried. By the time this photo was taken, in 1975, we already had been stirring up mischief for years. Somebody's gotta do it.

I said, "OK, Budwin. Anything that works for you tickles the shit out of me."

Meanwhile, Susan and I were falling deeper and deeper in love. She's the daughter of a West Texas cotton-farming family. With her rural background and my small-town upbringing, we both relished the "big" world, but we also appreciated being able to get away on occasions.

Our first Christmas together, Susan brought me home to the farm to meet her family. My arrival sort of liberated the male members of the Streits. Susan's uncles, close-cropped hair and proper manner, couldn't drink around family. At least not much. Well, I showed up and raised the bar a notch or two. They could now do anything they wanted, because the worst they could do still seemed conservative compared to me. Susan saw this transformation of her family relationships and just chuckled. One night we all took my Caddy for a ride in the pasture, top down, rolling through the fields.

Musically, I was working really hard at stirring the Gonzo stew. When the band and I were not traveling, we were working on a new album or staying up all night at somebody's house, hearing the new material that was being played around town.

As we were flying back from a gig not long after we had cut *Viva Terlingua*, I asked John Inmon what else we could possibly explore. He said, "Well, we haven't tried horns yet."

So we set up an audition for horn players at the Pecan Street Studios. All afternoon and evening, horn players trooped through. We would play anything that came to mind, and even some new stuff we were working up off the top of our heads, trying to see who could keep up with what we were trying to do. Tomas Ramirez and Jim "Squank" Baker were the last ones standing. So we looked at each other and said, "They must be the horn players."

Shortly afterward, we headed into the studio to cut the album that became *Walker's Collectibles*, an experiment with horns added, Tomas on sax and Squank on trombone. We used the same approach as the first two albums: keep it loose, but make it breathe.

I was juggling a lot of balls. I was winging songs. I was leading horns without charts. I was trying to play behind the beat. Letting things fall naturally, I left harmonies to the background guys.

Donny Dolan, the drummer, said, "I'll let you go as far as it can, and then I'll nail it down."

A young songwriter named Billy Callery had moved to Austin. Billy, Milton Carroll and I became like the Three Musketeers. Milton and I shared a love of Fred Neil-style singing, so we were always singing some Fred stuff late at night.

Billy Callery was on a roll of creativity. We used his "First Showboat" on the new album. Milton and I wrote "Salvation Army Band" (a little tip of the hat to the hard work they do). Then I just made up a song at the session off a line that Cookie DeShay, the barmaid, would holler at closing time: "All right, it's time to head for the OD Corral."

In the summer of '74, I worked *Ridin' High* for a spring 1975 release.

By now I was beginning to think that maybe we had stretched the Gonzo approach a little too far, so for *Ridin' High* I wanted just a little more control. We flew to Nashville and used a studio owned by Norbert Putnam and David Briggs, two characters who shared ownership of Quadraphonic Studio.

To tighten things up a little, we laid down some rhythm tracks. I put Gary P. and Bob Livingston on rhythm guitars. We sat in a circle, sang, and did harmonies; I figured the bass, drums and piano would take care of itself. This way I could get Bob and Gary's full attention, and they wouldn't have to think about looking down at their instruments.

It turned out to be a good record, our second biggest after *Viva Terlingua*. The idea worked so well we used it again on *It's A Good Night For Singin'*.

But the live gigs were the heart of our music. After *Viva Terlingua*, I had come to like live recording so much that I had Dale Ashby and Father follow us on two tours. If we worked something up at sound checks or in the dressing room, we'd be able to get it on tape that night onstage. We got a lot of good material that way: "One Too Many Mornings," a medley of "Sea Cruise" and "Peggy Sue," a live cut of "Mr. Bojangles" in New Orleans.

Viva Terlingua had catapulted us into sold-out venues around the country. We were filling 6,000-seat auditoriums and 8,000-seat coliseums night after night. Everywhere we went, when we walked out on stage, the crowd went nuts.

"Hi, Buckaroos . . . "

"Yaaaaaaaaaah!" roared back at us.

The night we played Lubbock, two brothers — real Hoss Cartwright types — came backstage.

One pushed back his hat and said, "You boys sure look like you're havin' fun. Me and ol' Ed here was just sayin', if we could play music and be in a band, we'd wanna play and look just like you guys."

We were getting it across! Just stroll out on stage and start playing, like it's an extension of where you came from.

Chapter 10

My cowboy period . . . Treasured days on the rodeo circuit . . .
The one and only Larry Mahan . . . Amazingly, Susan says yes . . .
On the road with Willie . . . Hondo's gone . . .

I had heard so many stories of people in the business who had been screwed that I guess I felt I ought to get my licks in before they took all my money away.

I grew up in a generation that had air raid shelters in their backyards, and we practiced drills of putting our heads between our legs at school to survive nuclear attacks. Therefore, a lot of us thought we might be dead before we were thirty-five or forty.

We had protested the war in Vietnam and had marched for civil rights. We had been in jail and had shit thrown at us while we marched. I had lived on the road five or six years, slept in the rain, and had emerged with an all-time hit song. What did I care about boundaries?

Maybe that was some of the thinking behind all the crazy stuff we did in the '70s.

*   *   *

The summer and fall of '74 was my cowboy period. I'm not talking about musicians wearing jeans and wide-brimmed hats and outlaw mustaches. I mean real cowboys, tough as rawhide and crazy as they come.

It started in December of '73 with Bud Shrake calling, bellowing that I had to get to Oklahoma City right away.

Shrake was writing a piece for *Sports Illustrated* on Larry Mahan, a twenty-nine-year-old rodeo rider who had won the title of All-Around Cowboy five years in a row. After a couple of bad years, Mahan was back in the National Finals at Oklahoma City, earning points for a record sixth title.

Most rodeo cowboys are lean, compact, intensely patriotic, lucky-shirt superstitious, rusty-pickup poor. "Yep," "Nope," "Yessir," "Yes'm." The typical bull rider, flailing atop a one-ton Brahma, resembles the average high school halfback, maybe five-foot-eight, 150 pounds.

Susan goes for eight seconds on top of Larry Mahan at the 1975 Cheyenne Stampede.

Back in those days, most rodeo cowboys would arrive for competition with just enough cash in their Wranglers to make the entry fee with a little left over for cheeseburgers. They would sleep in puppy piles, packed in cheap hotel rooms or wedged inside campers and pickup trucks.

They might win a few hundred dollars after an eight-second pounding ride on some huge, angry beast. Then they'd lurch into the dark, driving all night to the next rodeo town. Blue smoke trailing behind pickups and horse trailers, they'd leave like suntanned gypsies. Driving all night, listening to country radio, talking about their bruises and sprains. Counting up again all the bones they'd broken through the years.

Larry Mahan was different, a professional athlete. Well-spoken with great interviews for the television reporters. Injury-proof, broad smile, fun-loving.

"You've gotta meet this cowboy," Bud said to me over the phone. "He rides in all the events, wins everything, screws everything, flies his own plane. This guy's amazing."

"I'll be there. Where is it?"

"Oklahoma City."

So I went.

It was great meeting all the cowboys. Some played guitar, sang their own songs. Mostly, I enjoyed their camaraderie. These guys had been competing and traveling together for the entire rodeo season, and the best of the bunch had made it to the National Finals.

They had accumulated purses and scored points all over the country. The livestock they rode were all four-legged athletes too, earning points and making it to the Finals based on bucking style and performance.

In a riding event, when the gate opens, the cowboy can earn up to 50 points for the ride. The horse or bull is ranked by the judges on another 50-point scale, with both scores added together. Tough bull and you stay on, 82. Really tough bull and a perfect ride, and it's an 89.

Mahan was a three-event competitor, riding bulls, bareback and saddle bronc, picking up points for that all-around buckle and leading the rodeo cowboy image out of the dusty rural arenas. He was exciting, colorful, electric on television, easy to talk with.

We went to the Saturday night Finals competition and watched Larry win and do a couple of flying dismounts at the end of the eight-second ride. We headed for the hotel where everyone partied late.

The hotel bar TV hummed with the midnight sign-off for the local station, and the national anthem began to play. In unison, every cowboy in the bar rose to his feet, took the hat off his head, and placed it over his heart, without a word. The anthem ended, and the bar boiled back loudly, glasses clinking.

Mahan, in a gesture of friendship, took his lariat and looped it around my neck like a Hawaiian lei. I left the bar, working the hotel from room to room, feelin' real cowboyish. As the night dragged on, Gary Nunn from the Gonzo Band and Gary Cartwright, a writer covering the rodeo for *Texas Monthly* magazine, decided they were tired and were turning in.

We were partying strong in Cartwright's room, so I said, "Here, take the keys to my room. I'll never use it."

So off they went.

Somehow, in the course of wandering the halls, I wound up in a room with a cowboy named Bobby Steiner and a bunch of his friends. They were all egging me to take Bobby's guitar and sing "Charlie Dunn." Finally I did.

"Buck's makin' change
He never sees no one
And he never understood
The good things Charlie done."

"Buck," the old grump in the song, is Bobby Steiner's grandpa. We all started argu-ing over how grumpy he is, how I shouldn't put him down in a song. Then they start-ed shoving and punching me.

I took Mahan's rope off my neck and whirled it fast as I could, to keep them at bay. I backed out into the hall as somebody exited an elevator, and I sidestepped into it, swinging.

I headed straight to Cartwright's room, but by then only Shrake was there, watch-ing TV in bed. I walked in, all disheveled.

"Fuck a bunch of cowboys," I hollered.

A tray of dirty dishes went sailing across the room. No reaction from Shrake. I punched a lamp over behind a chair. Shrake glanced at me and then back to the tele-vision.

Shrake always carried this nasal inhaler filled with methedrine mixed with water that we'd use for a "lift" now and then. I threw the inhaler at the TV set. "Fuck rodeo, too," I yelled.

The inhaler did it. Shrake jumped up, "Last straw, Jacky Jack."

He threw the other lamp against the wall. We proceeded to trash the room. Totaled it, laughing, drunk and fried.

Our night's work done, we fell into bed there in Cartwright's room.

Dawn came and then noon. We arose amid the rubble and decided to get out of that savaged room as fast as possible. As we were easing down the hallway, we heard a maid behind us exclaim, "Aw, shit! They partied on my floor."

I turned and hollered back to her, "Yeah, you might as well plow that room under."

Gary Cartwright, we later learned, was informed that he was never again to set foot in the Oklahoma City Holiday Inn — unlike the delightful Mr. Walker and his group, who folded the towels before leaving.

I was so taken by Mahan that when the season started next spring, I told my office to book me into as many rodeo towns as possible. I could watch Mahan and get to see some of the other cowboys too. The parties where the pickin' went on were the best. The stories and the fellowship are something I'll treasure forever.

One of the first rodeos we played was the Calgary Stampede, the concert in the big arena. All the cowboys were there. Down in front was Doug Vold, son of Harry Vold, the biggest stock contractor in Canada.

Dougie hollered, "You gonna play 'Jaded Lover'?"

I said, "Sure, but come up here and sing it with me."

I reached down and pulled him up on stage. Dougie leaned into the mike, gave a little "yeee haaa," and then, through the PA system hollered, broad and full-throated, "Pussy!"

Every cowboy hat in the arena went flying.

We broke into "Jaded Lover," instantly a real, certified cowboy band. We closed the night with half a dozen cowboys on stage with us singing "Good Night Irene."

That night, Mahan and I switched hats as we left the gig. We climbed into his motor home, Mahan driving, and headed for the Sports Page bar. Along the way, we kept kidding about giving our hats back.

I said, "Mine's too shitty for ya I guess."

He said, "Well, that's my trademark hat."

I said, "I used to worry about not having a hat till I met a man who didn't have a head."

Everyone pondered that remark while I casually pitched both our hats out the window. Mahan slammed on the brakes, jumped out his door, and ran back to get our hats. I slid over to the steering wheel and drove off in the motor home with Larry's buddy, T-Bone Clark, laughing his ass off in the back. When he realized I was drunk and didn't know one thing about driving in Calgary, he said, "Circle the block. Let's go back and get Larry."

Careening through the streets, motor home leaning into the corners, I tried to get us back to where I thought Larry was. Of course, we couldn't find him. So we decided, "Hell, somebody's picked him up by now," and we headed on to the bar.

We walked in the door and there was Larry Mahan, a beer in each hand, wearing both hats.

I never worry about a man wearing two hats.

Later that night in my hotel room we all sat around singing cowboy songs, some old, some written by these guys themselves — T-Bone, Dougie, Larry, and the Gay brothers, Donny and Pete.

Finally Doug Vold gets up from his chair and raps his girl on the head with his cowboy hat. "Come on, Mama, we're goin' to the house."

She dutifully gets up, and that starts the exodus of cowboys groaning to their feet.

"Good night, Mama," to Susan.

"See ya tomorrow," to me.

Susan and I lay on the bed talking about how strange and funky all this rodeo cowboy stuff was.

There comes a knock at the door. It's Pete Gay. He comes back into the room kicking stuff, looking under the bed and in chairs.

He turns and says, "You know, it's the little shit I can't handle. Big shit I got. Give me a bull or a bronc, and I'm fine, but little shit like car keys, and I'm dead."

We finally locate the keys, and as he's headed out the door we hear, "Good night. Fuck it. It's always the little shit that gets me. See ya later."

All that summer and fall we rodeoed and sang and traveled together, ending up at the National Finals in Oklahoma.

Larry was thinking of retiring and starting a clothing line and maybe a singing career. We drifted apart, but kept in touch when we could.

Larry eventually wound up at cutting horse events and settled for a while in Phoenix. One night after a concert at Arizona State University, Larry picked me up, driving a funky limo he'd bought for cruising the town.

We headed for Mr. Lucky's. We danced with all the girls and took turns jumping up and singing with the band. We were having too much fun, I guess, because somebody outside threw a rock through the front windshield of that limo.

We were leaving Mr. Lucky's, windshield half gone, glass everywhere across the dash, a huge rock sitting on the front seat between us, when Larry spotted two good-looking Buckle Bunnies leaving together.

He yelled, "Hey, c'mere a minute."

They walked over, and Larry said, "You want to go home with a couple of real cowboys?"

They look inside. See the rock. See the glass. Look at him. Look at me.

"Fuck no!" and they walk off, rounded bottoms fading into the dark.

Larry leaned his head out the window as we eased out of the parking lot. "Had your chance," he hollered. And crunched gravel into the desert night.

We went back to his place at the edge of town, drank some beer and listened to interviews Larry had done with old cowboys he'd met during his travels. Great stories.

We sat there listening till Larry jumped up and declared, "Let's go ride bareback!"

See, Larry doesn't think anybody knows how to ride till they ride bareback.

There's something about first light in the Arizona desert. Two drunk cowboys, riding horses, in the best dawn of their lives.

*   *   *

I wrote Susan a song about the moment I asked her to marry me. It declared, "Susan you are a jewel/rarest I've ever seen . . ." and "The moon was so bright/I musta knocked out all of your lights/That's when you fell for my silvery line."

Most women go "awwww . . ." when they hear that line. Oh, but they do not know what Susan knows.

I had finished *Ridin' High*, and I thought we'd get married . . . maybe in Luckenbach.

She knew me pretty well by then, knew I was pretty much a rascal, hard-livin' and ramblin'. One night we were driving home to the house in Oak Hill, the top down on Susan's little Triumph convertible, the stars of Texas arrayed in majesty. We started down my bumpy, long, gravel driveway, and I slowed the car down and turned to Susan.

I said, "Well, I guess we oughta get married."

She said, "OK." One word. OK.

I exploded: "Hell, I thought you were smarter than that!"

I could not believe that this intelligent, strikingly beautiful woman would have the poor judgment necessary to hook up with me permanently. I yanked the emergency brake on the floorboard so hard, it jammed straight up. I started yelling and cussing, leaped out of the car, grabbed a tire iron and shattered both of her headlights. Then I stomped off up the driveway to the house, leaving my new fiancée slack-jawed, sitting alone in her convertible in the middle of the Texas night.

Susan started the engine, and despite a perpendicular emergency brake which she could not budge, she coaxed that chattering little Triumph through the dark to our house. I was pretty darn impressed with that pluck.

Besides, I had my answer, and I wasn't going to let her back out on it.

Susan had been with me to Luckenbach many times by then, and had come to see it as a refuge, just as I did. We called Hondo and asked if he would marry us.

With six-time World Champion Cowboy Larry Mahan during a photo shoot at Luckenbach, around 1990. Mahan may have been the first rock–and–roll cowboy. He dragged rodeo into the modern era.

The happy bride and groom with the wedding party in Luckenbach, December 12, 1974. No organdy bridesmaid's dresses, no polyester tuxedos, but a hell of a good party.

He said, "I could, but I don't think it'd be legal."

"Well, find us a justice of the peace, and we'll get married in the post office next Thursday."

He said, "OK."

There was a long string of cars as all the Mad Dogs and Gonzos headed for Luckenbach. I brought along a pickup full of champagne iced down in the bed of the truck.

We partied till the justice of the peace, Garland Taylor, said if we didn't get going, there might not be anybody sober enough to have a wedding. So as the sun set on a warm December 12, 1974, we were married in the store with Nadine Eckhart as Susan's best lady and Hondo as my best man.

It was one of the greatest days I've ever had, and the following couple of years became the happiest period of my life.

I finally felt as if I had found a home. I was where I wanted to be, doing what I wanted to do, living the way I wanted to live. I was making music that mattered to me, and it was finding an audience, reaching them and making them feel good, just as I intended. I was touring and coming home to people I loved.

Naturally, it couldn't last. Not for the Head Chef stirring the Gonzo stew.

*   *   *

In '74 and '75, our booking agents started packaging me on tour with Willie Nelson.

It made sense, since we appealed to different audiences at the time. I had released

Viva Terlingua and was pulling in a hippie crowd. Willie had just done *Red Headed Stranger* and had a big hard-core country following.

I remember a show in Jackson, Mississippi. Willie and I were sitting on the balcony watching the cars and trucks pull into the parking lot.

I said, "You probably got folks in the new pickups, and I've got the old restored models."

Willie sighed, "Or just the opposite."

Our first joint concert was in Baton Rouge. Willie, Jimmy Buffett, Jerry Jeff. Good show, then off to New Orleans. I was supposed to close the show, I guess on the strength of "Redneck Mother." Gary P. and I went to Willie's bus and said, if it was all right with him, we'd just as soon that Willie closed the show. He had all the right to be the headliner, and we were young bucks with a lucky hit.

Willie said, "If that's what you want, OK."

After "Blue Eyes Cryin' In The Rain" there was no question — Willie was the headliner.

But what I remember most about that gig was the governor's mansion. Edward Edwards, the governor of Louisiana, wanted to meet Willie. To be nice, he also invited Jimmy and me to the mansion.

I didn't remember the invitation until the phone rang in my hotel room in New Orleans the morning of the show. I'd been up partying all night with the locals.

The governor's office had sent an officer in a patrol car to drive us to the mansion

From around 1976, when Jimmy Buffett and I both had more hair . . . Willie still has all of his, the lucky dog.

in Baton Rouge. We were running late, so Susan and I hopped in the car and took off. We were to pick Willie up at the New Orleans airport and bring him with us.

At the airport Billy Cooper, Willie's aide-de-camp, walks out and says, "Hello, Cuz. It's your cousin Billy Cooper. Fast Eddie ain't gonna show."

Willie being a no-show was not new, and he had been nicknamed "Fast Eddie" for his dropping in and out of parties whenever it suited him.

I said, "Climb in, Cuz. We're off to the big house."

Susan, Billy and I raced on to the mansion, stopping every now and then to dash into a bar to pee, do a blow, and scarf down a beer.

We screeched up to the mansion with Jimmy standing on the steps. As I stumbled from the patrol car, Jimmy said, "Tuck your shirt in and let me do the talkin'."

Susan handed Jimmy a gram, "This will help you talk, wise guy."

We had time to kill so we took pictures of Susan and me in some Mardi Gras king-and-queen crown and scepter we found there.

In the Governor's Mansion.

When we joined the governor for lunch we were all so jacked up we didn't eat a bite. And we all talked at once.

Finally the governor said, "Could I get you some coffee or dessert? Or Valium?"

Billy says, "Now you're getting warm, Gov."

The governor had other business to attend to so we adjourned to the parlor and proceeded to drink his beer and wine.

Some ladies from the Daughters of the American Revolution were coming to the mansion, and security wanted us out of there. To entice us to leave, they offered to deliver four cases of beer with us to our hotel.

"OK, let's go."

Well, the band was partying in my suite when I got there. In short order it was evident there was not enough beer.

"Let's go back to the mansion."

So I called and said we were planning to come back because we were running out of beer.

Security told me they'd deliver more beer if we'd just stay in the hotel and not come back.

They did.

Willie and I toured quite a bit together then. We also played a lot with Emmylou Harris. So Bea Spears and Rodney Crowell and I were always pickin' at the hotels after the shows. Bea was, and still is, Willie's bass player. Rodney sang harmony and backup vocals with Emmy and wrote several of her top songs.

People were always prowling the hallways of the hotels looking for parties. Once somebody stuck his head in our room and said, "Who's in here?"

Rodney said, "Just the same old happy faces." He was right; most nights it was the same faces playing new songs.

We started chartering planes to get to the gigs. I never could ride the buses very well. They call that "livin' in the tube." Planes allowed us to stay later and leave the next day.

There was an early charter for those who wanted to go to sound check, and a late plane for me to arrive a little before show time. I hated to get to a gig and just hang around waiting to play. I still hate it. I want to walk in, feel the energy, then hit the stage.

I liked Willie, but opening for him didn't do much for my creative energy. We were only playing 45 minutes, for a crowd that was mostly Willie's, so I didn't feel a lot of incentive to be creative. Nobody was listening to our stuff much, anyway.

And I have to admit, my own lifestyle on the road didn't make for the sharpest performances either.

I hadn't been very productive as a songwriter during the past year or more. The last song of mine I had recorded was "Pissin' In The Wind," the final cut of *Ridin' High*. The next album, *It's A Good Night For Singing*, which we cut in Nashville in late '75, included none of my own work.

Not long after *It's A Good Night For Singing*, the Lost Gonzo Band got its own deal with MCA Records. I had to look for a new band. I didn't much like the idea, but I had to face the fact that they might be touring on their own.

It had been a pretty hectic three years, and it had started to unravel there at the end.

Gary P. Nunn, who had been instrumental in forming the Lost Gonzo Band, helped me put together a new band. I was gathering up people I had met while touring the past couple of years.

Freddie Krc had started drumming with me in the final days of the Lost Gonzo tours, and he stayed. Tomas Ramirez came along, too. Ron Cobb, on bass, joined me from Colorado. He had been with Michael Murphey, but wanted to try something different. Cobb also played sax, so he and Tomas could play brass together on the records. Bea Spears thought I would enjoy working with Bobby Rambo from Dallas. And we had guitarist Dave Perkins along with Reese Wynans on keyboard.

I called this group the Bandito Band.

The Bandito Band, from the *Red, White, Blue* album.

We left on our first tour, with Dale Ashby and Father following us. We did some spotty live recording, but the best stuff was from a live show in New Orleans. I was booked into a new concert hall just outside the Quarter. We rode a horse and buggy to the show and cut quite a few things that night. I invited David Briggs, Norbert Putnam, Kenny Buttrey on drums and Weldon Myrick on pedal steel to join the band on stage. I called them the "four on the floor."

Unfortunately for them, I decided during the show to do different songs than we had rehearsed together in Nashville a day or two before. During the encore I noticed that Briggs was not on stage with me, but in the audience with his arm around a girl, and he was throwing pieces of paper at me that he'd had his notes on. I hadn't played any of those songs!

We came back to Luckenbach to cut some more live stuff, then went back on the road.

That's when I got word that Hondo had passed away from a heart attack.

I was stunned and confused.

I got drunk for a week and missed the funeral. Truth is, I didn't want to go anyway. That was to admit that his death was real. This way I could think he was still around.

144

I kept missing him, thinking, "He'll show up any time now."

I didn't go back to Luckenbach for ten years.

My band was leaving and Hondo was dead. Life was swirling around me.

The live material from New Orleans and Luckenbach became the core of the new album. I included some poems from Charles John Quarto, who had lived at the ranch with Hondo for a time. Bobby Rambo and Bea Spears and I pieced together some songs as a tribute to Hondo. Eventually I had enough material for a double album, which I called *A Man Must Carry On*.

That project ended with Willie joining us somewhere on the road for a live version of "Will The Circle Be Unbroken." Good question!

It sure felt broken for me.

Chapter 11

Contrary to ordinary ... The Honchos de Soul ... Late for Chattanooga ... And messing up another birthday ...

Though some of us had already worked on the album *A Man Must Carry On*, the Banditos actually pulled together as a real band in Lafayette, Louisiana. Rambo, Cobb, Wynans, Perkins, Krc, Leo LeBlanc and I all came to the home of Bobby Charles Guidry, a Louisiana character who wrote the hits "Walking To New Orleans" and "See Ya Later, Alligator."

We had a concert planned at the college in Lafayette. So we flew in early and got hotel rooms, and drove out to Bobby's to rehearse. He had a buddy named Bird who cooked all day while we sang and drank beer and worked on songs. Alligator stew and Dixie beer, too.

Some nights we never made it back to town, just slept on the couch or in a hammock on the porch. We jammed this way for about a week — a fun time, and we got to know each other and how we'd approach songs.

I asked Rambo where he thought we ought to record the next project. He said, "We always make good music in your house out in Oak Hill."

So that's where we went, with Malcolm Harper's mobile studio parked outside and playback speakers in the living room. Susan was now pregnant with our first child. She and a Louisiana girl, Cheryl Petre, cooked gumbo in the kitchen while we made music in the "Guy Clark Memorial Music Room" at the other end of the house. It was a fun time with fires in the hearth, music throughout the house, cooking smells from the kitchen.

We found that the old upright piano in the music room was out of tune by about half a tone low. With the mobile studio running on a clock, we didn't have time to get the piano tuned, so our new keyboard player, Reese Wynans, improvised on the fly by transposing everything down a half step. He never really learned the songs in the right keys.

The album included two songs by Bobby Charles and one of Rambo's. We did a song I had learned from a Ringling Bros. clown named Billy Jim Baker. It was "Contrary To Ordinary," which also became the title of the album. The back picture of the album is me wearing clown makeup as a guest clown with the circus.

Contrary To Ordinary is one of my favorite albums.

We had fun recording it that way, and it came through on the record.

Then it was off on what became the infamous "Willie Cold Weather Tour," a lunatic plunge into the powerful winter of 1978. On this tour, the backstage passes were a laminated picture of Willie wearing earmuffs. We went through Minnesota, Wisconsin, North Dakota, Kansas and Iowa in the middle of winter, late January and the first two weeks of February.

Half of the dates had to be rescheduled. Snow, heavy snow, everywhere. We were stuck in motels, city after city.

We got stuck in a Holiday Inn in Madison, Wisconsin. Our band took over the stage in the hotel bar. They called themselves the Honchos de Soul.

I was helping the bartender make Brandy Alexanders. The whole dance floor was sticky from spilled drinks. Customers and band, snowed in.

I didn't even like hotels! Especially hotels full of crazy musicians. The guests, stuck there too, acted just as crazy as the bands. The gigs we did make were just big-assed parties with the few locals who could manage to get out of their houses. We eventually flew home to finish recording.

We were definitely "contrary to ordinary."

We finished the album, mixing it in Nashville and ending with a wrap party at the Jim McGuire Studio. Jim was the photographer for most of the album cover shots during this period. We listened to the final mixes at his studio, then went on the road again. This time, south.

We were playing mostly in the Atlanta area. I was flying as usual, but each day I would have to go back through Atlanta to change planes. It was taking twice as long to get around as the bands who rode buses.

I spotted a '54 Lincoln four-door hardtop in a used car lot. I bought it and christened it "The White Whale." Bea Spears and I started driving to gigs. It had a tube radio and no power steering. Not the quickest way to get around on the winding little country roads in north Georgia and Tennessee. We almost missed one gig, and Willie pulled Bea out of the car. Grounded. "No more riding with Jerry Jeff."

Two dates later, I missed my opening gig in Chattanooga. The White Whale led me on some swirling backroad trek, and it took forever to reach Chattanooga. Because I hadn't showed up yet, the promoter told the audience I wasn't going to make it, then instructed the security guards to stop me if I drove up, because then he would have to put me on and pay me.

The White Whale came sliding up to the arena. I immediately walked right past security and headed straight on stage, up to the mike, and fell in singing with Willie. The promoter glowered from the wings. When Willie wrapped, everybody walked off stage to thundering applause, and then walked back for an encore.

Everybody but me. As soon as I stepped into the wings, I was arrested.

My birthday was the next day, and I was in jail. I was going to keep alive my record of fucking up on my birthday.

So I started the day in the Chattanooga jail. That night at the Nashville gig, Mama Mae Axton presented me with the key to the city. I was thirty-four.

The Gonzo Air Force, circa 1977 . . . this is your captain speaking, along with your cheerful and courteous attendants: Steve Keith, Susan Walker, Gary P. Nunn and Bob Livingston.

Chapter 12

The Super Bowl all night long . . . Defining obnoxious . . .
Princeton's loss, not mine . . . The 'wild' period takes its toll . . .
Susan's content . . .

For much of the '70s, I was literally on the road more often than I was at home. In a typical year, with about 200 gigs, I would spend about eight months in hotel rooms and in airplanes getting to them.

We flew everywhere. After the first time we'd flown on charters, we never wanted to travel any other way.

We instituted a rule. Any gig two hours' flying time from New Orleans, we went to New Orleans!! "The good news is, you're in New Orleans; the bad news is, you're up all night."

The other good news is, "It don't matter."

In 1976, Willie and I were invited to come to Miami and play the Super Bowl party for the Dallas Cowboys.

Susan and I flew to Miami in a Piper Navajo flown by Dr. John Young and his wife Patsy.

Somewhere between New Orleans and Miami we hit a huge line of thunderstorms. We were bouncing and bumping our way along for at least half an hour. The tower said there was no break.

I suggested we land and go to a bar.

John says, "No, no! We'll punch through here somewhere."

A small plane against a big storm is no match. We were like a rag doll in a Doberman's mouth. We made it through, but I was cold sober by that time and proceeded to change that.

We went to the Fountainbleu Hotel for a pre-party. Bill Murray and I sang "Hang On Sloopy" and other classics. As the party wore down I decided to look up some old friends in "the Grove."

A party ensued there as more and more old friends came out of the woodwork. Before I knew it, kickoff was a couple of hours away.

Susan was with the Cowboys and their entourage, leaving Fort Lauderdale at noon. And she had my ticket. I knew I'd never get there in time, so I headed straight for the stadium and bought a ticket from a scalper.

Consequently, I wound up sitting on the chilly side of the stadium in the middle of the Pittsburgh fans. As I looked across the field, I saw the whole Cowboy section in the warm sunshine.

Susan had given my ticket to the bus driver, and he was sitting beside Clint Murchison, Jr., the owner.

I didn't dare cheer for the Cowboys because I was afraid some Steelers fan would beat me up.

I walked down near the end zone to get some sun, and the punter had his punt blocked at that end of the field. The Steelers front four smashed into the fence right by me.

At that point I'd been up so long, I'd jump at my own shadow. The collision with the fence made my heart leap right up into my throat.

The Cowboys lost 33-31.

At the Cowboys' after-party at their hotel I played a few songs. I was taking the loss real hard, but for the veterans on the team, life goes on.

Blain Nye consoled me by asking me to show him some chords. It helped.

The 1980 Super Bowl in New Orleans would be a lot more fun.

*   *   *

We used to get three or four rental cars. The band would drive them all up to the front of the rental agency while I went through the paperwork at the counter.

"You want the dollar-a-day insurance?" the agent would ask me.

"Oh, yeah, we want that."

"Did he get it?" the band would ask, grinning.

And all of a sudden, out in the parking lot, you'd hear this "bam, bam, bam," and the band and roadies would start backing the cars back and forth into each other.

We'd get four contracts for the cars, and four maps showing the way to the gig. I would walk out to each car and say, "Here's your map and your stuff."

And we'd all holler, "Gumball!!"

We'd all blaze out of the parking lot in different directions, a race to see who could make it to the gig first.

After we played we would head out to a bar. After the bars closed we would drive home drunk every night at two in the morning, somebody throwing you the keys to a rent-a-car you barely remembered, heading into the night to try to find a motel where you've never stayed.

Bobby Lemons, our roadie, got pulled over for coming out of a club about two-thirty in the morning in Mississippi somewhere.

"OK. We saw you comin' out of that bar, weaving. You shouldn't be drinking and driving."

"But you don't understand, officer," Bobby said, indignant. "We do this for a living. We do this every night somewhere."

He straightened up, chin high. "I'm a *professional*."

*   *   *

Hotels and I have had some rough times together.

I was in some city — Los Angeles I think — and got back to the hotel after partying at somebody's house. The desk clerk was waiting for me.

"You're gonna have to leave."

The hotel was saying that Susan had been "loud and obnoxious" in our room.

"We don't do a lot of obnoxious things," I started to explain.

"Hey, I know obnoxious when I see it," the guy said to me. "We've had too many complaints tonight."

I said, "No, obnoxious would be somebody who would do something like this . . ." and I took a wastebasket and kicked it. "Like this!" And the wastebasket, in a perfect punt, sailed up and over the hotel counter.

"Now, *that's* obnoxious!"

The clerk just stood there, frozen.

"But we're not those kinda people," I said, in perfect preacher voice, and went to get my stuff from the room.

*   *   *

I was in New York to work on a project, and Bud Shrake asked me to come over to the offices of *Sports Illustrated*. The editor gave me Bobby Orr's hockey stick. I was feeling great, and Bud suggested we take a trip to Princeton University to visit Larry L. King.

Larry L. was teaching as writer-in-residence at Princeton, and he was having a faculty party Friday night.

Sterling Lord, Bud's agent, got us a limo. Bud, Murph and I headed for New Jersey.

The campus at Princeton is old Ivy League. The grounds are immaculate; the party was stuffy, wine and vodka. I took the limo driver and went to get three or four cases of beer.

After the driver and I loaded the beer into the kitchen the party jumped a notch. Voices got louder, the arguments more vociferous. The general tone got more pushy. Soon Sterling said he had to get back to New York. He had only expected to spend two or three hours there.

Larry L. told us he had a rental car from the university. We could drive it back to Manhattan and drop it off. We turned the limo loose and proceeded to party on.

Leaving New Jersey for New York in Larry L.'s rental car, I was telling more stories, and Murphy started complaining that I can't drive and so on. We argued all the way to Manhattan. At a red light in the Village she jumped out and caught a cab to the hotel.

Bud and I went on to Elaine's. She was about to close, but let us in. Bud introduced me to Elaine, and when she found out that I'm an old bartender, she invited me to help close up.

153

We closed Elaine's, and I dropped Bud off at his hotel. I was looking for a place to park when I decided to check out a porno flick in Times Square . . . at six in the morning! Pretty deserted.

I parked in front of a porno house and walked in. The movie must have been slow because I dozed off. About 9 a.m. I woke up and hit the bright sunlight. Honking cabs and busses and cars everywhere.

But no rental car! I cabbed it back to the hotel and crashed.

It took my office three days to track down the car. It had been stripped and towed somewhere up above Harlem.

Princeton was very uptight about the car. Larry L. nicknamed me Jacky Jack Double Trouble from that point on. Gosh, I was just checkin' it out.

Lost the hockey stick and probably won't be invited back to Princeton either.

Their loss, not mine. I've done that already.

*　　*　　*

Somebody gave me a box of amyl nitrate ("poppers") for a wedding present.

We flew to Barbados. I had always wanted to go to some exotic place. Had to take about a half dozen planes, seems like we just flew forever. I was just ripped out of my gourd. Amyl nitrates, airplane drinks and toot.

Susan was completely pissed at me when we finally got there, about midnight.

When we got to the hotel for our honeymoon, we checked into separate rooms.

The desk clerk was rather amazed. "Never quite had this before, for a honeymoon."

We stayed a week at some huge resort, then found a quaint house. Swam in the ocean. Ate conch, pumpkin fritters, fresh fruit, fresh fish. We were going to be there for about a month, so we called Guy and Susanna Clark in Nashville and asked them to come join us.

That's where Guy first sang me "Coat From The Cold," which he had just written.

At the resort, I kept trying to get the house band to play local music. They were playing "Yellow Bird" and crap like that. I told these guys, "Get loose, play what you play around here."

And this woman barked, "What do you know about music?"

"Oh, I'm a songwriter."

"Well, why don't you get your funny cowboy hat and play us some of it."

OK. I played a few songs, smashed my guitar, and we left.

The guitar was a rosewood Gibson, a type which now sells for about $20,000. I made a statement for the sake of art.

Guy Clark, who makes guitars by hand, went back with a shopping bag and picked up all the pieces.

As a friend says, "The dogs bark, and the caravan moves on."

I called Guy a couple of years ago — about twenty-five years after Barbados — and I said, "I'm thinking about getting a pick guard. You still have those pieces of the Gibson?"

Guy saves everything.

"Yeah," he said. "You could make that, or a real little ukulele."

So he found those pieces — yes he had them — and made a pick guard out of that rosewood for my '59 Telecaster.

For a while there I had a terrible thing about breaking guitars. I must have broken about six in that period. The Angel on that birthday years ago in Key West. That rosewood Gibson, the wedding guitar. One of them I broke trying to make a point. I had it by the neck and banged it down onto the floor, too hard. The neck went right down through the guitar. There was one other, a twelve-string.

Somebody said, "Don't let your music kill you."

That was the last one.

Oh, I think I threw one in a fire somewhere, but it was a cheap one.

*   *   *

I did a tour in Australia — Foster's Beer, methedrine, and powerful vapors.

One night the Gonzos and I were in this sailors' bar in Australia, and they were selling "Rush" — butyl nitrate — over the counter. We were there having plenty to drink when a lovely young thing at our table purred, "Buy me a Rush."

"What's a Rush?" we asked. Before she could answer, I hollered, "A round of Rushes for this table here."

I'm not quite sure when the room flipped end over end, but I know it didn't take long. Around that time we realized that the young lovely with us was a transvestite.

Sort of fit right in with the rest of that upside-down night.

Cobb and Tomas went off with some biker gang, and were presented with this pile of white powder on a table. Tomas figured it was cocaine and just popped his nose down over it and snarfed up a whole snoot full. And of course, it was biker meth. They said his cheek just melted down his face. I don't think he slept the whole time we were there.

Now they were all wide awake forever, and we were supposed to do a TV talk show, sort of the Australian version of *The Tonight Show* hosted by an American stand-up comic who had been there for a dozen or so years.

As we were doing our sound check for the television show, Tomas showed up wearing a pork pie hat, flip-flops, a shirt that said "Eat More Shit," and these terry cloth sweatpants he'd been wearing so long they had a permanent outline of his dork.

The stage manager told him, "Tape it down."

Tomas answered, "Bad taste is timeless."

I was wearing my jogging pants, T-shirt, a camel hair sport coat and a cowboy hat.

"Now, straight from Texas!

"Jerry Jeff Walker!"

I stepped through the curtain, and there was this little snicker from the audience. The drummer hit a little rim shot.

I bowed and tipped my hat.

The host asked, "Are you enjoying Australia so far?"

"Well, we've been here 48 hours, and I don't think we've been to bed yet!"

Our last stop on the tour was Adelaide, my favorite city in Australia. Beautiful river, laid-back, barefoot hippies, folks who got what we were all about.

We played the concert, and afterwards we were shaking hands with folks from the audience. Among them were two guys holding a fellow who was completely passed out.

They said, "Write something on his forehead. He's your biggest fan. He got drinking so much tequila before you came on, the second you sang 'Hi, Buckaroos' he passed out. And he missed the whole concert."

So I wrote, "You missed it" on his forehead.

They dragged away my biggest fan, his feet scraping down the hallway.

We all adjourned to the hotel bar to teach the bartender to make upside-down margaritas.

*   *   *

The height of the "wild" period was '72 to '78. It seemed a lot longer because we squeezed so many hours into each day.

Albums, touring, partying, writing songs, putting together bands, marriages, babies, and breakups.

I was getting older in a hurry.

When Susan became pregnant, she decided to hop off the train. She was making a list of her priorities, and number one was the baby on the way.

Susan seemed so complete. She was calm and contented. She had purpose in her life, and it showed. I was envious. I wanted to feel that too.

But I wasn't there yet.

One the road with the Bandito Band in 1979 (that's guitarist and songwriter Bobby Rambo in the background). As you can see, the road takes its toll.

Chapter 13

Jessie Jane arrives . . . The mud hits the fan . . . Hello, Uncle Sam!
. . . Susan makes the change . . . Time to go home . . . and sleep . . .

Contrary to Ordinary was my seventh album for MCA. Beginning in '71, I had cut and released one every year. It was a good, steady relationship that had survived despite serious changes in FM radio that potentially affected the audience for my music.

FM had always been free-form; a disk jockey could play what he liked. If his knowledge of music was good, he attracted a following. He usually built his reputation with his own collection of records on top of new things coming out. If you had a "different" album from most, you made sure that those DJs got your record. Since I had never been a Top 40 type of performer, the independent-minded FM DJs were the base of my popularity on the radio.

Over time, though, those loose stations began disappearing, purchased by big conglomerates which had a play list handed down by programmers and consultants. Individual tastes got pushed aside, and more often than not, my music didn't fit the format. Since I had followed my own head, I had gotten farther away from mainstream. But I did have a cult following, and that was good enough for MCA.

I had wanted to stay with MCA; we were working together fine. But Warner Brothers' Elektra label, coming off monstrous hits by Fleetwood Mac, was floating in money and had gone on a talent-acquisition spree. They signed me for three albums, for more money than I had ever before been paid.

That spring Jessie Jane was born; April 10, 1978.

I had mixed emotions.

Proud of a beautiful daughter.

Pressured to be more successful.

Trying to guide this motley crew of managers, roadies, bandmates and entourage down the road.

Turn and go in a different direction? Or crank it up?

Some of those feelings show in "She Knows Her Daddy Sings." It's about love for Jessie, but it's also talking to Susan.

"For Little Jessie" (She Knows Her Daddy Sings)

Sometimes out here on the road
Too late to call, I see the telephone
My mind's a line running straight for home
I think I see her sleeping soft and warm

CHORUS:
> *She knows her daddy sings*
> *We know all that the money brings*
> *She thinks our world is everything*
> *But does she know*
> *She's the precious thing?*

I know we've had our ups and downs
Drove our love nearly out of bounds
Can't go back to a lot of towns
We were doing what was going' round

(Repeat Chorus)

Well, two adults in a world alone
We'll take a little love, make a little home
The little hands touch your wavy hair
Then wave goodbye and leave us standing there

(Repeat Chorus)

She thinks our world is everything
But does she know she's the precious thing?

I went to work recording *Jerry Jeff* as the first of those three albums for Elektra.

By now, the lifestyle of playing, singing and partying had become nonstop. We all flew to Miami to record at a studio in Coconut Grove. Bad move. Flush with more money than we had ever known before, we found ourselves in an area awash with cocaine, and we were in a crash-and-burn frame of mind.

So for two weeks we piled into Bay Shore Studio in Coconut Grove. The studio had no feel: it was very big, very cold. Those two weeks seemed a lifetime, and the only thing we got done was staying pretty well fucked up all the time, everybody. We got one song out of it all, Mike Reid's "Eastern Avenue River Railway Blues."

Freddie Krc was just back in Austin from this trip when he ran into a friend on the street.

"Man," said the friend, "you look terrible. Where've you been?"

"Miami. For two weeks. Never saw the light of day."

We cut the rest of the album at Pecan Street Studios in Austin, but it was still crazy. Too many people, no direction. I was tired and blown out, and my voice

Jessie Jane and Dad in Paradise — specifically, Kauai, Hawaii, back in 1981.

sounded like it. I had no approach. I was just setting up and playing anything I could think of.

Jerry Jeff was a hodgepodge of songs just thrown together. "Lone Wolf" was the high point, a Lee Clayton song about a lone wolf coming to town — "lock up the women and hide." I had a real fondness for "Follow," a Jerry Merrick song he wrote when we all lived in the Village.

Those weeks in mid-1978, I would drift, thinking about our new daughter. The rest was wearing me out. I spent all my time stoned and either on the road or recording. Sleeping in cars, waking up at gigs, stumbling into the studio. Growing a beard, wearing polyester so the wrinkles wouldn't show and nobody could tell how long I had been up.

It was a collision course. We had all this money and we were also playing our asses off, working about twenty shows a month, staying up all the rest of the time.

For three months, Susan and I separated.

She had embraced motherhood, totally cleaned up from her own hearty years of partying, and she wanted those people out of her life and out of her house. The druggies and the hangers-on weren't welcome at the house at Oak Hill, and I qualified on at least one of those counts. When I wasn't touring, I was living out of a car, moving from place to place.

Then it really hit. American Express sued me for $90,000 in unpaid bills. We had been flying everybody first class, racking up massive hotel bills, commissions to agents. Once we lost a rental car, just flat forgot about it. Left it parked two months in some Sheraton parking garage way back down the road. That cost me $5,000. Would have been cheaper just to buy the damn thing.

American Express was amazed. They were trying to figure out how we had run up a tab like that in just a few weeks. Usually, the company spots charges building up and shuts down access to the account.

I was spinning my wheels. The faster the money came in, the faster it went out.

Then Uncle Sam showed up, saying, "Where's mine?" The IRS wanted a look at my last four years' tax returns. And they didn't want to talk to some lawyer or agent. They wanted to talk to me.

The wolf was at the door.

I was desperate, and I didn't understand where all the money had gone. I saw myself running ragged while management and booking agents took fat commissions off the top. Meanwhile all the expenses of making the music came out of my end. Seemed that once I got finished paying studio fees and the band and all the travel expenses — planes and rental cars and hotel rooms and all the rest — I was actually making less money than the guys who ran my career, sitting in offices and making phone calls.

I felt as if I was pulling a long train with too many people.

This had always been true, but the big deal with Elektra had actually accelerated the spending. A contract with a bunch of zeroes at the end gave the illusion of prosperity, but when the money you're spending exceeds the amount that's coming in, you're in a hole, regardless.

I thought that management could've done a better job of looking after things. But in the end, it's my life, my money, and I had been spending both real hard without much thought to the consequences. After fifteen years, fifteen albums, 200 shows a year, my life was in a shambles.

During the lawsuit and the IRS settlement, I saw how it was all going down. I decided to make a break. I was scheduled to do another record for Elektra, but I'd do it myself and take my chances on the street.

One of the tracks opens with me saying, "This is the last song I'll ever record here." The Pecan Street era was over. I did it as wild and loose as I could. I knew things were coming to an end.

I cut a lot of stuff that had been rolling around in my head, some of it even recorded by myself, alone.

I called it *Too Old To Change*. The title was ironic. The day after I walked out of the studio, I gave up drugs, whiskey, cigarettes and red meat.

I went home to Susan, and I slept.

Chapter 14

Wake-up call: Hello, this is Jerry Jeff . . . Down to beer and pizza . . . Django joins the family . . . No birthday disaster at forty . . .

I was eating salads and soups and fruit smoothies, just getting my bearings, physically and mentally. I started trying to run to the mailbox a half mile away, breathless the first few tries. A friend handed me a book on juice fasting. It was two weeks until my thirty-seventh birthday so I fasted for two weeks.

I have never been half-assed about anything that mattered to me, and this time what mattered was turning my life around. The old Gonzo approach still prevailed: take it to the limit, and then a little farther.

And it was working. Things were clearing up. I needed a rebirth that came all the way down to the cells. Since 1978, I have fasted seasonally, and when I sense a break point in my life or career, between something ending and something beginning, I fast again.

I started spending part of every day with Don Smelly, a partner of my manager, Michael Brovsky. Smelly was my link to the working of Brovsky, and together we began to figure out what I owed the IRS. We had to prove I wasn't intentionally defrauding the government. Somebody as loose and carefree about money as I was is not scamming to defraud the government.

It was a big-time wake-up call.

We were poring over the books of the last few years preparing for the IRS. Smelly was staying up day and night to piece it all together. We needed receipts based on touring. We had to back up bills with facts. I was getting cleaner, and he was getting deeper into how I used to live.

I came face to face with some hard truths about the music business.

It works like this: you're a guy with a guitar who writes a song that becomes a hit. You think you've got it made, but your troubles have just begun.

You start to live the way you figure stars should live. Room service and limos, groupies and parties. You pay for every cent of this, whether you realize it or not.

Occasionally, your management team comes out to see how you're doing; they fly first class, stay first class, and charge it all to you.

They also keep you working and on the road every minute possible — hey, that's their job, and they're getting a cut of every gig. Between the playing and the traveling and the partying, you don't have a lot of time to catch up on the details of how much money you're spending and how much is going out.

And your management won't make a big effort to let you know these details. It's in their interest to be somewhat vague. Because then you depend on them; your life is in their hands.

"Trust me" might be the most commonly used phrase in the music business.

Nobody cares about your best interest more than you. You'll never get that kind of loyalty by paying a percentage.

The fact is, there's a built-in conflict between a manager's interests and an artist's. Even an honest and scrupulous manager isn't interested primarily in how your life is going. His basic function is to keep you out there working. It doesn't really matter to him that most of your gigs are being played to cover taxes and expenses — he's first in line when the checks arrive, taking his cut off the top, and he doesn't really care where the money goes after it leaves his hands.

Then you wake up one morning remembering your kid back home: "God, I missed another birthday."

As I spent time with Don Smelly, going over the records from the past few years, I realized that I had cared nothing for money, and that other people had taken advantage of that and had gotten me in trouble with my own money.

I realized you absolutely must look after the money or it will definitely get you in trouble. You can't pay somebody else to do it because they don't really care. Ultimately it comes back to you. All the bills, all the expenses, all the canceled checks . . . they're yours.

I promised myself once I got this done, I would remove myself from this path for good.

It was a long fight, through daily meetings with the lawyers. Finally we worked it all out. I paid, I didn't go to jail.

To settle with the IRS, I refinanced my house. And then I found out MCA wanted a new deal. They had released *The Best Of Jerry Jeff Walker* in 1980 and had done well with it.

Elektra Records still had me for one more album, but they could save big bucks by not making that record. They paid me to call things off —a hundred grand, enough to pay off American Express. That cleared my way to sign again with MCA and start a new project.

I was turning around the rest of my life, too. I knew that Susan had talked to lawyers about a divorce. I thought, "Shit, if we get lawyers involved, they'll get it all." I told Susan that if she wanted a divorce, I'd just give it all to her and Jessie Jane. But it turned out that wasn't necessary. Susan was behind me, if I was going to live and live healthy.

And I was. After three months of fasting and running and regular rest, then eating better, I looked and felt years younger.

It was during this period that the solo work I was doing came together.

The family on the hill in Oak Hill: Susan, Django Cody, my ownself, and Jessie Jane, sometime in the early 1980s.

My son, Django, was born, and I attribute his good health and solid behavior to his coming along at this time in our lives. Susan and I were making a conscious effort to live healthier. Hell, I was running five miles a day and drinking carrot juice!

One night, watching Monday night football and drinking beer (carbo-loading, in runners' terms), I showed Steve Fromholz how the juicer worked. I fired a couple of slices of pizza through it, it covered the whole kitchen wall — he was impressed. Susan said from now on we would have to be chaperoned while watching football on TV.

But that was the extent of the craziness. A good time for me now was beer and pizza and a run the next day.

* * *

In 1981 I went to work cutting a new album for MCA. I had let go everybody in the band and the entourage except Bobby Rambo. He and I flew to Muscle Shoals, Alabama, to start the album with Barry Beckett and the Muscle Shoals Rhythm Section. I called this project *Reunion*.

I thought it was a good title for someone coming back to himself, my own "reunion." It was fun and very professional, not in the Gonzo fashion, but an album of quality, as good as I had ever made.

Seven of the songs were mine. A few were rerecorded, but I thought we brought new life to them. Barry Beckett was a great producer, and Bonnie Bramlett was a joy to sing with. I thought it was a good effort, but it got lost in the MCA shuffle.

I still had one more record to make with MCA. I flew to California and met with Jerry Weintraub. He was John Denver's manager, and Neil Diamond and Bob Dylan had just signed on with him as well, so I thought I'd talk with him.

Bert Zell, Jerry's partner and manager of the Pointer Sisters, thought I should put together the best band I could find and tour some, get solid songs together and do a knockout album.

So we did. I brought back three of the Banditos. Reese Wynans, Rambo, Cobb and I were the nucleus. Cobb brought along a wild man from the '60s Byrds, Michael Clark on drums, and a young kid named Mike Hardwick on guitar and pedal steel.

I was trying to lead the band in laid-back but structured ways. I started playing a nylon-string guitar for a softer, folksier sound. I think by then that I'd lost every other guitar I ever owned.

I celebrated my fortieth birthday with an all day concert on Auditorium Shores in Austin. For once, there was no birthday disaster. In fact, it was Texas heaven.

We started the day with a four-mile run ending at the concert stage. I finished the run, had a beer and walked up on stage and opened the show. Every half-hour a different band would play, and the show went from noon till midnight. It ended with fireworks and "Hill Country Rain."

We rolled into *Cowjazz* with a pretty good feel. We weren't as wild as the old Gonzos, but we also weren't as tight. It takes years sometimes for a group of musicians to blend or "breathe" together.

We cut the album at Willie's Pedernales Studio out in the Hill Country.

Producer Larry Butler flew in to see if he could work with this band and if the studio was adequate. Butler was a highly regarded producer, most famous for all the Kenny Rogers hits.

This was a time when videos were coming in, and I didn't do one. MCA decided not to put any support behind this album and just sort of shelved it.

The last song of the session was "Wind," a Bob Bruno song from our first Vanguard record when we were Circus Maximus. I had come full circle. "Wind" was the last song I would cut for a major label.

You good lookin' sumbitch, don't you **EVER** die . . . Onstage at the Livingston, Montana Music Fest in 1976, on a bill that included Jimmy Buffett and the Nitty Gritty Dirt Band.

This was shot from the phenomenally successful "Don't Mess with Texas" anti-litter campaign in the late 1980s that featured Texas musicians, athletes and celebrities.

Chapter 15

'We're all just dancing chickens' . . . How the music business
screws the talent . . . Susan takes charge, conditionally . . . Gonzo
Airlines flies again . . .

After this last attempt with MCA and dealing with Weintraub, whose office was on Rodeo Drive, I really felt I was done with California and major labels.

Someone once told me that "Colonel" Parker, the manager of Elvis Presley, started out as a carnival barker, staging an act called "Dancing Chickens."

He would take your money, let you inside the tent. There you'd find one sorry chicken on a platform. Hidden from view was a hot plate, which the Colonel would turn on, forcing the chicken to jump around, lifting one foot and then another.

Fred Neil, the talented songwriter who was screwed about as many ways as it is possible to be screwed in this business, told me once, "You know, Jerry, we're all just dancing chickens."

In the summer of 1985, I jumped off the hot plate.

After a run of three or four months in '82, *Cowjazz* had gone quietly away. For about three years afterward I toured with the musicians from that album. I went from one manager to another, working steadily, paying the rent, but not really satisfied with the music.

I wasn't happy with the direction of my career, either.

I had no albums in print. The record business was in limbo. The CD — compact disc — was on the horizon, ready to replace vinyl records and cassette tapes, but it hadn't happened yet. Record companies braced for the transition, holding back old stock, waiting for some breakthrough album by a major artist like Bruce Springsteen to be released on CD only. That would do it — people would buy CD players to hear the new product.

Until then, the whole industry was treading water, and sales were low. Companies weren't signing artists, and all the old product was out of print.

The manager/booking-agent crap was getting old for me, too. I was playing the same places year after year. I could book them in my sleep.

When I started sitting down with accountants, I realized that one year I did $467,000 worth of business and I spent $400,000 doing it. That profit, $67,000, represented about eight gigs. The rest was the cost of doing business.

I had never even seen a lot of it. A booking agent takes 10 percent of every gig up front. A manager gets between 20 percent and 50 percent depending on his ego. At 50 percent you may as well marry him or her. Randy Travis did. Many husband-wife teams wind up managing each other.

Once a performer becomes successful, two things happen, both of which favor the manager and the booking agent.

First, their commissions get a lot bigger. That's because they're now taking a slice of a much bigger pie.

Yet at the same time, their jobs become much easier. Once an artist is established, booking agents and managers basically answer the phone and sift through offers. In other words, they're doing less work for more money.

A hell of a deal. And they're not the ones spending half their lives in hotel rooms. Agents and managers get to go home at night.

My booking agent, Bob Engel, had been a constant good guy in all the years of booking. He kept me busy and he put up with some jerky managers, most of whom were not good for me. But Bob kept me working.

I wasn't sure that most of the other people who had been taking big cuts of my income had been earning their money, though.

I was so frustrated. Shit, go on the road for two months, come home, and after everybody takes their cut and you pay the band and the bills, you barely have anything left.

Then, a great revelation.

Susan informed me she was going back to work. The kids were starting school and, she said, "Working every day is what people do."

I told her that if she wanted to work, she ought to go to work for me. Be my manager, my booking agent. Not only would this instantly reduce our overhead, but I would trust her the way I had never trusted my managers before.

She had one condition.

"If I do run your business, we're not dealing with any assholes, OK? If I say someone is a jerk, I want you to believe me, because why should I lie to you? I love you."

I thought that made a lot of sense. And I loved her, too.

I guess I'm the only asshole she continues to do business with.

She fired the manager, who seemed to have more of our checks than we did, and took him to court to recover the paperwork of our business. When we got it, we saw all his expense accounts. Flying to L.A. on my behalf, staying at posh hotels, limousines, expensive dinners.

And we had to break down the band. Had to personally tell them that we were not going to keep doing it. Bands break up and go their separate ways — musicians know that work is a precarious thing — but this was still tough.

It takes a lean dog to run a long race, and Susan and I had decided that we were in this for the duration. Stripping down to basics wasn't just an economic decision, though; I also felt instinctively that the time had come to start over.

I had to have all these music people, managers and agents and producers and hangers-on, just go away and leave me alone.

I had to find my own pace and my own head. I needed to get enthusiastic about playing and singing and writing. I needed to play and have fun in front of an audience I could talk to and share the music with.

Back in the '70s, we had crossed over into big-time concerts, big amps, big arenas and stadiums, with the audience stuck hundreds of feet away. It's not about music that transports you someplace else. It's an event — the event is cool and you're there and it's exciting. There were a lot of us doing a lot of the same things, and when everyone does the same thing it gets ruined.

My hero, Yogi Berra, once said, "Nobody goes there anymore, it's too crowded."

Chet Baker, my musical hero, said, "The world I come from and how we played music is gone. They call it progress."

Drugs allowed Chet to block out the bombardment of the modern world, so that he could sink into the space between the notes. He said, "Heroin was a foregone conclusion to how people like me were going to try to play the music we wanted to make."

They sacrificed themselves to be able to concentrate and lose themselves in their music.

Music is as much a mystery to the artist as to the audience. We don't try to control it, but ride with it. A lot of things have to happen right in order to get loose and be free enough to enjoy the ride.

All the people you play with must get on some mutual wavelength. Great bands bring to the stage a respect for each other, a love of playing, a childlike joy in getting lost in the music. They find something fresh to look for each time you play a song.

Chet Baker said, "I like my commitment to the music to tell my fellow musicians, 'Here's where I will go to. Meet me there.'"

The leader of the song must establish a mood, a character for all the rest of the musicians to follow.

When I finally got back to playing solo, that's what I found: myself, in the middle of the song, total concentration. Lost in the lyrics and letting the music create the mood.

I would return to that by playing solo.

I had to quit so that I could begin again.

*   *   *

Susan has this sign on her desk: "If it has tires or testicles, you're gonna have trouble with it."

That's Susan. Not that she isn't sweet and lovable — she definitely is that. But when the time comes to do business, she can be tenacious, tough and uncompromising.

We started with the idea that we'd argue about business during business hours and live our personal lives the rest of the time. Raise a family and run a business. Susan is very good at doing behind-the-scenes work so that artists can have their freedom to do what they do.

An incident from 1989 pretty much typifies the way Susan approaches business.

We'd recorded *Live at Gruene Hall*, and Willie Nelson had dropped into one of the overdub sessions and laid down a track for "Man With The Big Hat," a great song by Steve Fromholz.

We wanted to use Willie's voice for the cut. Willie said, "Aw, don't worry about it, don't tell anybody, just do it."

Right. Like nobody will notice Willie Nelson singing on our album.

Susan sent a letter to the president of CBS Records, Willie's label. No response. She sent a fax. Nothing. Phone calls, follow-up letters, absolutely no response.

"Look," she told the Nashville offices on the phone, "just tell me yes or no. I'm waiting on you to put this record out."

Couldn't get an answer.

Well, Susan went to Nashville for some recording industry seminar. Whenever she had to endure one of these obligatory gatherings, she'd pretty much get trashed.

And there was nobody better to help her with that task in Nashville than Harlan Howard, a songwriter who has written more classics than anyone left standing.

Harlan — tall, leathered, no bullshit.

Susan and Harlan tucked arms, and together they began to make their way together through all the parties and gatherings, getting merrily smashed along the way.

They were standing in the midst of one party, snagging drinks off trays that passed by. Everybody was wearing name tags. In the middle of making small talk, Susan happened to notice one name staring up at her, "Joe Blow, President, CBS Records."

Susan reached over, grabbed the man by his necktie, and hauled the astonished record exec right up to her face. "You're just the sumbitch I've been lookin' for."

He was petrified.

"Who are *you*?" Mr. CBS said.

"I'm Susan Walker. I've been calling, I've been faxing, I got this Willie Nelson duet, I want a fuckin' answer and I want it *now*."

As Susan walked out with Harlan, he told her, "You scared that poor guy to death."

"I thought I was pretty nice," she said.

"You speak with your eyes," he told her.

The incident didn't do much for Susan's reputation in Nashville. Or maybe it did.

Live at Gruene Hall album liner notes end with the notation, "Willie Nelson appears courtesy of CBS Records."

That's the way Susan operates when she gets serious, and in 1985, she was on a mission. She sued to get back our financial records, sued to recover money owed us.

A former business associate told me, "They don't call her Sue for nothing."

"Yeah," I said, "but we only call her Sue when we do."

We were on our own, learning as we went along. Susan began to call William Krasilovsky, the man who'd written the landmark book on the industry, *This Business of Music*.

For a while there she was calling him at least once a week, begging for help, asking questions.

Bill Krasilovsky had no time for chitchat. Susan would tell him her problem, he'd quote a page number of his book and then hang up without even saying goodbye.

But the answer was always there.

We solidified our business structure. Groper Music continued as our publishing company, we formed Tried & True Music as our record label, GoodKnight Music ran things and Tried & True Artists handled bookings. The phone numbers for all these enterprises rang at a desk inside our home and office in Oak Hill.

Soon Susan aimed me out on tour, standing in the door smiling, her arms folded. I went down the road, just me, my hat and my guitar.

I can't say that it was easy at first.

For years, I had been a wild guy leading a crowd through some experiences, not really bringing them into the music. Being on a big, high stage with a band gives you a pretty good way to hide. Oh, yeah, we've all seen these hat acts come through the arenas with their videos and smoke bombs.

But I had started as a singer and a songwriter, a guy with a guitar, and now I was going back to the beginning. Now I was going into halls of a few hundred, sometimes tiny clubs with a few dozen people, sitting about eight feet away. I think there's nothing more in-the-face for an artist than to go out and sit in a room that close, that tender.

You don't just play. You talk about the songs, choose 'em, play 'em. And when the song ends, you have to be in the moment, because there's no place else to go.

Once I got all that going, I came to like it. My playing and dynamics improved, and I got back in touch with the audience, learning how to move them emotionally, to keep them laughing and crying and singing.

I liked this new way of traveling, too. I would get on a commercial flight with my guitar and some books. After the show, I would go back to a hotel room and write something by myself. My material became quieter and more introspective.

I spent about three years playing solo again. I would plug my guitar into every monitor and piece of PA equipment they had, and I became one big voice and guitar. I played small clubs and big ones. I'm the only artist ever to have played solo at Billy Bob's Texas in Fort Worth, the largest honky-tonk in the country.

At one point I had four gigs in Wyoming and Montana. I damn sure wasn't about to buy any more old cars to drive to gigs. In order to fly to each venue, I would have to keep going back through Denver to change planes each day. So Susan found a charter plane out of Jackson Hole, Wyoming.

Enter Lane Bybee. He was flying Turbo Commanders for a mining company in Riverton, Wyoming, and occasionally he chartered the planes to make extra money for the boss. When he found out that I was looking for a plane, he said "I'll fly him for nothing. I'm a big fan."

We worked it out that Lane could fly me to those gigs, and we had a great time. Lane also picked a little guitar and had a real positive attitude. He was western-lean and tanned, his pale eyes smiling, wrinkling with some story or remembered mischief. Little-boy eyes, innocence somehow preserved.

At the end of the run, he turned to me and said, "My wife is from Texas, and she wants to go back. If I can find you a cheap enough plane, would you want to use it?"

I knew that it would have to be real cheap to pass muster with Susan, but I told him to put together some numbers and let us think about it.

Two weeks later he called from Dallas. He had found a Piper Navajo for $130,000, nice and clean, about ten years old. He said, "Some other guys are looking at it, but I'm gonna test fly it to Austin, and if you like it, they can't buy it if I have it in Austin."

Susan and I drove out to the airport, and Lane took us for a flight. We liked it and called our banker, explaining what I spent on travel every year and how this would make it easier for me to get from Austin to wherever I have to be, whenever I wanted to go. I would add gigs because I could get to them more easily.

No problem. The banker said yes, and just like that, Gonzo Airlines is flying again. We named the plane "Scamp I."

So I'm off playing solo, Lane and me. Captain Bybee, he fuels and flies. I picks and lies, and we're all over the country. I bring some golf clubs. I felt after all of this running and jogging I was in shape for something, so we both started playing with fans who invited us to their country clubs.

Around this time, I met Danny Britt, a bright young golf pro at the Hills of Lakeway in Austin. He mentioned that he was also a CPA, doing taxes for lots of the golfers in Austin. I could hire Danny to do my taxes. He could travel with me, keep receipts, and give me lessons too — tax deductible!

He was tired of being in the pro shop all day, so he took a year's leave and joined our tour. We played great golf courses. At my shows, he and Lane sold hats, T-shirts, albums. Lane flew and Danny kept our books. My PGA-CPA.

I was having fun again, finally. I even got a gig in Augusta, Georgia, so we could be in town for the Masters. As we were flying around America I got to thinking. There were three extra seats in the plane. Why not put Bob Livingston, John Inmon and Freddie Krc in those seats? They could fly with us, same gas, same plane, and we'd make a stronger show.

I called the guys and everybody was ready for this. John Inmon had been playing with Delbert McClinton and Omar & the Howlers, and wanted a change. Freddie Krc had been in a band called the Explosives, but the gigs were thinning out. Bob Livingston had spent two or three years on an ashram in India and was now looking to get back into the Austin music scene.

I needed some new music to sell at shows, so we decided to cut a cassette. I got Malcolm Harper to bring his Reel Sound recording truck to my house in Oak Hill, and I started calling old friends. We sat and played stuff we hadn't done in a long time — sober, never. When we finished, I called Jim Rooney in Nashville and decided to mix at Jack Clements' studio.

We got some more pickers together there and recorded a bunch of stuff to round out my first album in four years. We called it *Gypsy Songman*.

This was the debut of Tried & True Music, my own label.

We decided to do only cassettes because they were convenient for people to buy at a show and carry home in their pocket or their purses. *Gypsy Songman* had been out on cassette for awhile when suddenly CDs took off. Rykodisc, a new company in the Boston area, had begun putting out a CD-only catalog of old material, starting with Frank Zappa and David Bowie. They heard *Gypsy Songman* and contacted us; we put together a deal by which they would publish a CD of *Gypsy Songman* while becoming distributors for Tried & True.

I was back in the record business.

Chapter 16

So much for a major record label . . . Susan builds our fabulous
fan base . . . 'Life's too short to ride ugly horses' . . .

There are certain rules for success in the music business. You must be on a major
label. You must get airplay. If you have both of these, then booking gigs is easy.
Booking agents can tell promoters you're on RCA and have a Top 10 record, and therefore you must get X amount of dollars.

That's why artists put so much faith in their producer and their label. They need a
hit if they want steady work.

They would eat glass to get a hit.

But that wasn't me. I had never been a monster-hit type of artist. I preferred to
make the music I wanted to make, figuring that it would find an audience if I did it
right.

When Susan took over the business, I was through with major labels. I knew it, but
Susan was not yet convinced. She wanted to explore a record deal in Nashville.

I had been through that circus before, and knew what would await us. But I wanted her to see it firsthand, so when she set up an appointment at MCA, I didn't argue.
I just went along.

We showed up at the offices of Jimmy Bowen, the head of MCA Records. Much of
the history of the Austin music revolution had been carved into MCA vinyl.

Bowen had his feet up on the desk, listening to what we had to say. Chunky little
fella. Beret on his head, beard, never took those feet off his desk. After a while he said,
"Give me some time with this. Let me smoke a joint, listen to your tape, and see if I
can figure out a formula."

He grinned, "Let's see if we can get you on some country-music radio."

My jaw closed way before Susan's. She was aghast.

"Excuse me, did you just say you were gonna 'figure out a formula' for Jerry Jeff?
Is that what you just said?"

Her black eyes darkened hard as bolts. "I don't want you to figure out a formula
for him. He's already figured that out. I just want you to put his records out."

End of discussion. That summed it up for her. Susan saw the inside of the music business. That's the way they think.

For Susan, that was final. We had no more discussions about deals with major labels. There was no way we were going to be able to accept Nashville, no way they'd accept us.

"I don't want to talk to them," she said, "I don't want to have dinner with them, I don't want to have drinks with them, don't want to be at a party with them, I don't want to ever be around these people again."

We didn't ever again discuss cutting a deal with a major.

The psyche of an artist is fragile.

He works with only his instincts to try to express some basic emotion. He plays or shows his work to some close friends. When they are supportive, he is encouraged.

He finally ventures out into the real world trying to play or sell his work to make enough money to have time to create more art.

He runs head-on into the commercial world of big business. They jerk the artist around to get him at the lowest cost.

This is "good business."

Since the artist isn't a businessman, they draw up a contract that basically screws him out of his money. He won't figure it out until he tries to pay his bills.

If an artist has pride, he cannot stand what is happening to him.

He hardly relates to this business world anyway, and he has little in common with the bosses.

Finally he just walks away.

We all lose.

This is why socialism has appealed to so many artists: "Give me an income, and I'll give you art. No fuss, no muss."

Capitalism says you must fight and make it to the top.

Luck and the ability to take a lot of crap from assholes is really what it takes.

I have been lucky.

To The Artist

This song is a letter sung
To a special friend of mine
One who stopped his singing
Somewhere back along the line

I wondered if he'd had enough
Of the rip-offs and the jive
Or did he sing his song one night
And lose the will to write

It never was a business deal
This thing with your guitar
It always seemed more a dance
Done deep down inside your heart

Tonight I wonder if it's true
Like we felt it at the start
That an artist truly does it best
When he does it from the heart

It seems to be much more than art
When the art you sell is you
Be careful how you play the game
Or else the game plays you

In the old days we'd stay up nights
And laugh until we cried
You said songs don't belong to us
We just bring some thoughts to light

The rule of thumb is never give
The truth away to rhyme
And a man can't lie when he tries to sing
It betrays him every time

We really write to understand
More about ourselves
And if we're lucky maybe then
We touch someone else

Well I just got back from Europe, friend
Where they hung on every word
It made me feel a little better
About my chosen line of work

They asked me if I knew if you
Wrote a lot these days
I told 'em all I know
Is that you rarely ever play

We start out singing what we like
And just give it all away
And wind up hating what we play
And sit begging to be paid

So let me say in closing, friend
I want you to know
I understand how hard it was
To let your music go

An artist must decide which parts
To leave in and take out
And if he no longer plays the game
That's what the game's about.

Susan understood that this is how an artist feels. She had an idea how to create an environment for me to make my music. She knew I had a hard-core fan base.

My music had touched some people very deeply.

She thought, "Let's find out how many."

She started building up a mailing list of fans who would buy our music and come to clubs where we played if they knew about the date.

It started with a sign-up sheet at the concession table at concerts. Then others wrote to us from a mailing address on the albums. It gradually grew.

We put the fan list in a database. I knew how to make records. Susan learned how to get them distributed. People found out where we were playing through the fan newsletters we put out quarterly. We got independent distribution. Occasionally we would release a single to get some airplay, but radio is hooked into the major label concept.

We made some noise, but mostly my career for Tried & True has been based on fans finding us, and on us staying close to the fans.

It takes a lot of work, but Susan built a staff that could do everything. Book gigs, arrange travel, keep records, pay taxes, pay bills, pay royalties — even promote gigs when there was no promoter to book them.

Susan created all this through Tried & True Music. She developed her own insight into the business, and it has proved to be right on the money. She tries to make each promoter aware of what we can do to support the act. We give away no backstage passes — ticket sales make money.

We have a great promotional tool in our fan club base. We advance the shows and help with the publicity. We choose the right people to work with, and we don't go where we are not wanted. We just adopted the policy to "go with the least resistance." If people don't want to do it, don't force it.

A publicist said to me once, "Gosh, you only go to the cool places."

"Yeah, life's too short to ride ugly horses."

I know that when I go to gigs, the promoters who have dealt with Susan tell me what a joy and pleasure it is to work with someone so personal, so fair and honest. It makes me want to hold up my end of the deal.

From my perspective, having a group of musicians who can move easily and lightly in any direction — renting equipment, using other bands' stuff — is also a blessing.

Bob, John and Freddie are willing to play on equipment that they aren't familiar with, but which they also don't have to haul around.

We aren't about equipment, we're about making music. We became a mean, lean, flying machine. We started saying, "We're paid for the travel; the music is free."

Keeping the business in the family didn't just mean saving commissions. It also allowed me to have something that resembles a normal family life. When your wife is your booking agent, you don't find yourself playing in Buffalo while your daughter is having her sixteenth birthday party back home.

One year I got an offer to play Detroit for $10,000, nice money, but it was near Christmas. I also had an offer to play in Hawaii at the same time; less money, but it would include rooms and airfare. We took the Hawaii gig because the kids were out of school for the holidays and could come with us.

If I'd had another manager, I never would have heard about the Hawaii gig. And I'd have missed another Christmas with the kids.

So we're raising a family and running a family business. A lot of balls in the air. Trying to work and be considerate and fair to everyone. To make a living and have a life where concerts and recordings and rehearsals co-exist with birthdays, ball games, graduations, anniversaries.

Keeping the business in the family and putting the family ahead of the career is the only way I know to do that.

It gets a little hectic with phones ringing, UPS guys using your toilet, rehearsals during dinner, but that's the way an artist lives. I still disappear to Belize or New Orleans once in a while just to goof off. Gotta goof off just to feel normal — no schedule. Hanging out has always been what I do best, and it's where song ideas come from. Susan's job is to keep me on time and as together as possible.

She has the work ethic that you would expect from a small-town Texas girl. While keeping business and family running between the lines, she found enough spare time to become president of a theater group in Austin and serve on its board of directors for ten years. At the beginning of the Austin music scene, Susan was involved in working with the City of Austin and was one of the first members of the Austin Music Industry Council. She served as entertainment coordinator for Texas governor Ann Richards' campaign and inauguration, and was nominated for television's Cable Ace Award for a concert video she produced at my Birthday Concert at the Paramount Theatre in Austin in 1990. She has been involved with both Live Oak Theatre (now the State Theatre Company), and the Paramount Theatre.

If I didn't drag her off on some wild fling now and then, she would probably work all the time. She's a mean bridge player, too.

Sometimes I have to sit back and wonder how I ever was lucky enough to marry someone so grounded.

To top it off, she's also beautiful. Well, she is beautiful in many ways, but also in the way most people mean when they use the word. I mean real easy to look at. She's a knockout, always has been, still is.

A few years ago, we had a party at our house. Crowded room, lots of conversation and laughter. Out of the corner of my eye, I caught a glimpse of a stunning woman way across the room, with her back turned my way. Made me stop and stare. She turned to me, and I saw that it was Susan.

At that moment, my heart did little things. Right there on the spot, I fell in love again with Susan. Yep, all those years later.

So I wrote this song with Don Schlitz, "Last Night I Fell In Love Again," and sat down with a guitar on my lap and sang this song to Susan for the first time.

Last night I fell in love again
And I didn't think I could
I thought by now I was probably

Over that for good
With too much on my mind
Too many things to do
Then last night I fell in love again with you

When I finished, Susan looked at me, paused and said, "Jerry Jeff, what are you guilty of this time?"

"Nothing but loving you," I said.

*　　　*　　　*

When I began planning my second album for Tried & True, I remembered the energy and spontaneity we had gotten on the live recording for *Viva Terlingua*.

I had played an old dance hall down by New Braunfels, Gruene Hall (pronounced "green"). I thought this might make the perfect setup. I gathered musicians in Austin who could rehearse, and got in touch with Malcolm Harper to use his mobile truck again.

I had earlier taken the *Gypsy Songman* tapes to Nashville to add a few songs and work with an old friend, Jim Rooney. I had enjoyed working with Jim. He had encouraged me to follow my head and play what pleased me.

Now I wanted Jim to supervise the Gruene Hall recording session. Someone needed to be in the control room making notes about certain takes, to tell us which takes felt good and which ones we should do again.

The concert taping was a cold December night in 1988, and the old dance hall was chilly. I asked everyone not to drink during the first run-through so that the audience didn't peak too early.

The first run was sterile, no life. I said into the mike, "We'll take an intermission, and the whole band will join you at the bar."

We had a couple of beers, went back to the stage, and shot right through each song. By now, everybody in the house had some idea of what the songs would be like, and they warmed up in a big way. That second set became the album.

One of the best things from the Gruene Hall project was working with Lloyd Maines, who played pedal steel. Lloyd was a major figure on the Lubbock music scene with Joe Ely, and also his own band, the Maines Brothers.

Lloyd has a real easy way around the studio and has great respect from his fellow musicians. He has patience, a great ear, and a real feel for what the songwriter wants out of the accompaniment.

I rounded out the band with Paul Pearcy on drums, Roland Denny on bass and Champ Hood on guitar. Brian Piper from Dallas played piano.

From *Live at Gruene Hall* we put out two singles written by Chris Wall. One was "I Feel Like Hank Williams Tonight," which I did on the Leno show while he told how tough his life had been. The other was "Trashy Women," which got mixed airplay and caused a fuss in country radio due to its lyrics and raucous theme. Screw 'em if they can't laugh! I was still stirring the Gonzo stew. We put out a couple of albums of Chris's songs to thank him and to turn our fans on to his music.

All this got enough attention that MCA released a compilation, *Great Gonzos*. I was

On the eve of recording the *Live at Gruene Hall* **album . . . I love the way they dress up the old town with Christmas lights, wrapping the water tower and the windmill, and hanging the wreath above the old dance hall. It kind of puts the human scale back in the holidays.**

now in the CD arena by fluke, with three CDs out when most country acts had none.

Tried & True Music was solid now. The fan club was up to 40,000 names and growing. We were a cottage industry to be dealt with. It wasn't important enough to threaten anybody, but Susan and I recognized that we had something of real value. I could play and create music, with the freedom to do what I wanted. We could tour and support a band, and we would keep all the money at home.

Maybe most important, I was surviving — as an artist, as a businessman, as a human being.

Popular music in the '90s seems to be about who sells the most and who has the most outrageous videos.

I think it's important to find out who is still standing. My goal is to not be on VH1 as one of the great tragedies of all time. That's too easy, and I refuse to do it the easy way. If there's anything you don't want me to do, just go ahead and tell me to do it!

*   *   *

Live At Gruene Hall is still the best-selling album in the Tried & True catalog. It would have done even better, but I never got to do a follow-up tour because my back gave out. I had been running five miles almost every day for six or seven years. I didn't do much stretching, and I was constantly tightening my back.

I'd had back problems as a kid. I was real skinny and probably injured it falling off of everything I'd jumped onto.

I also caddied as a kid. I would carry some doctor's big-ass bag for a three-day weekend, sometimes two bags. When I went to play Pine Valley years later, the caddies took all our clubs out of the tour bags and put them into lightweight nylon bags. I thought, "Smart guys!"

I was X-rayed, and they found a broken vertebra, #5 above the pelvis. I would need fusion, bone chips from the hip hanging across 4 and 6. A pretty big deal. I would be laid up for two or three months.

So 1990 was mostly recoup and rehab. I was really starting from scratch again. To have major surgery knocks you down. You're never the same.

After surgery, I started recovering by inching along the driveway every day with a stroller. I put a squeeze-bulb bicycle horn on the handle bars, honka-honking when I needed help. I ate a lot of chicken soup. Slowly I got to where I could use the whirlpool at the country club, and finally I got to where I could take off the brace and go swimming in Barton Springs, the famous spring-fed swimming hole in Austin.

I wrote about it in a book called *Barton Springs Eternal, The Soul of a City*:

"In the early '70s, all I knew about Barton Springs was that it was a great place to recuperate from a hangover and watch pretty college girls in skimpy bathing suits. By 1980 I was looking to shed a few pounds and change my lifestyle somewhat, and a friend, Bill Swail, said, 'Let's go jogging on the hike and bike trail and end up with a swim at Barton Springs.'

"It was like finding an old friend. I would run three or four times a week and swim every time. In the winter you run first to get hot; in the summer you swim first to get cool, then swim again after the run to cool down. Nothing like it.

"By 1987 my back was bothering me so much I had to stop running. After lots of deep massage and lots of adjustments, the touring and golfing and years of not stretching caught up with me, and I had to have back fusion surgery. I spent two and a half months flat on my back, then the whirlpool and slow walks to get myself going again. Through it all, in the back of my mind was Barton Springs.

"Finally, in April, I took my kids, Jessie and Django, and we made the pilgrimage to the springs. I took off my back brace and slid into the pristine waters. With the kids walking along the wall above me, cheering me on, I swam the length of the pool. At the far end I stood up with my hands high over my head and yelled, 'I'm back! I'm back!'

"I've heard over the years that the Indians of the Hill Country called it the Sacred Springs and would come there to heal their wounds.

"So do I."

That first full lap down the length of the pool was great. The kids were on the bank cheering me on. I made it, and I knew I was on my way again.

Chapter 17

Lo and behold, ten years of stability . . . The Gonzo Compadres . . . Adios, Scamp I . . . Playing for the president . . . The breezes of Belize and order in the Quarter . . .

After decades of surfing the seas of chaos, turning life upside down and shaking it to see what would come out, I looked around one day and discovered that I had found stability.

I'd lived in the same house for twenty years. I had a family, a beautiful wife and two growing, healthy kids. I was playing the music I wanted to play, with a business and a career that was rolling along.

Now, I don't want to mislead you into thinking that it was all that sedate. After all, insecurity is my security.

But as I write this, mid-1999, it's been ten years since my back surgery, ten years without upheaval, ten years during which I've found a lot of happiness and satisfaction in my home and family, my career and my music.

Ten great years during which I've been happy with where I am, who I am and what I'm doing.

If you're now checking out the pages remaining in this book, and thinking that ten years are going to go by in a hurry, you're right. Contentment doesn't provide nearly as much drama as crisis and craziness.

Sure is a lot easier on the nerves, though.

*   *   *

The first gig I played after my back surgery was in Minneapolis, at the Guthrie Theatre, solo. Nine hundred seats with me and a guitar. I played two hours standing in a back brace. I felt awkward, but the crowd was listening, and I was so glad to be performing that it became a magical evening. After all I had been through, there I was standing alone with a guitar, telling stories, and singing the songs that I'd been compiling for years.

It was time to get the band together and start touring again.

We'd just started playing and traveling again when one day, flying on final approach into

Dallas' Love Field, I saw Lane Bybee shut off the right engine. We landed, but the engine burst into flames as we were taxiing to the terminal.

"Stop the plane. We're gettin' out of here."

We pushed open the door, grabbed our guitars, and jumped to the ground. A fire truck was pulling up to douse the flames. I stood there thinking, "There goes my little plane."

The paper the next day reported that Jerry Jeff Walker and his band "scampered" off their private plane amidst smoke and fire.

Scamp I was history.

Insurance covered the repairs, but we traded it in for a Turbo Commander, closer to the plane Lane first flew me in.

We also started on a new project, *Navajo Rug*.

We used the studio at KLRU-TV where the *Austin City Limits* show is taped; it sits vacant all summer long. They had all the equipment of a full studio, plus a big sound stage. We could set up shop in Studio 6-A and record for a couple of weeks there. The room has been fine-tuned acoustically. It has a nice dry quality. It was close to home, with lots of room, and was available.

Performance shot from the mid-1980s at the Fairmont Hotel in Dallas.

We were working in a big open sound stage with monitors and a big snack table and coolers of water and sodas. We set up in a big circle, all facing Freddie Krc's drum kit. We had vocals and some guitars and pianos in the monitors, and it gave it a homey feel.

I chose "Navajo Rug," an Ian Tyson/Tom Russell song, because it had all the qualities of a good country song. Strong woman, a sense of humor, and a nice tie-in to a Navajo rug that the waitress and cowboy made love on.

Also, we got a lot of play out of a song titled "Nolan Ryan (He's A Hero To Us All)."

I was teaching my son, Django, how you could take a story like Nolan's career and build a song around it. Ryan had just pitched his sixth no-hitter and was approaching 5,000 strikeouts. So I wove together a tale of a small-town Texas boy "who can bring it" through his years with the amazing Mets, to the Angels, through the Houston Astros to the Texas Rangers.

We flew to Dallas and premiered

the song in the dugout with Nolan listening. Django was bat boy that day, and we made news in *Beckett Baseball Digest*, a magazine which Django used to get to follow all the baseball card news.

It was a fun father-and-son thing to do. It also represented the way I like to use songs, to take something that's a part of our lives and put the experience to music.

Django had a good time with it, and soon he started playing guitar. I'm not sure how serious he is about it, but I hope he finds something he likes in music. Personally I don't care if he does play music for a living, but if he does, that'll be fine too.

He's a good, decent boy with a great head on his shoulders, and I'm sure he'll do just fine. I hope he travels the world and has a great life.

He's my hero.

*   *   *

Within a year, I was back in the KLRU studio. Brian O'Neil of The Nashville Network asked me to host *The Texas Connection*, a new TNN show.

The idea for the show was that country acts, mainly from Nashville, would appear and play live on the soundstage while they were on tour in Texas. I added an interview portion during which I tried to bring out some of the personality of the guests.

Kris Kristofferson, Willie and I kicked it off. Later we had the Texas Playboys, then Jimmy Buffett and I sang and told stories about Key West days. Vince Gill, Trisha Yearwood, Steve Warner, Mary Chapin Carpenter and Mark Chestnut. I had Hoyt Axton on one show, and Guy and Susanna Clark with songwriter Richard Leigh. I really wanted the show to follow songwriting more, with guitar pulls and a friendly relaxed talk with the guest.

Nashville called the shots, and it never quite became what I had in mind for it, but later it did become the blueprint for the Ricky Skaggs show broadcast live from the Ryman Auditorium, the old Opry building.

In show biz, you play the hand you're dealt, and then you move on.

I did get to find out that many of the singer-songwriters were influenced by the stuff we did in Texas early on.

Vince Gill, Nanci Griffith, Mary Chapin Carpenter, Steve Earl and Garth Brooks all said they listened to and sang my songs when they were starting out.

I learned that many people thought they'd try music because of the fun, loose stuff we did in the '70s.

I like the idea that we followed our instincts and that others coming along will do the same with their music.

*   *   *

In 1992 I decided to get involved with the presidential race. I felt that with the deficit so high and Social Security and Medicare in doubt, the Democrats were the best hope.

I had learned during the Vietnam war period that you have to get involved to change things. The Republicans are about big business, and they admit it.

I'm for the rest of us, OK?

Early in the Democratic race, I liked Senator Bob Kerrey. I had met him and liked his direct approach. Somehow he just didn't click early, and his campaign was over after the

Another Texas Connection episode, from 1992 . . . this is the perfect Texas trifecta, from my point of view.

New Hampshire primary. I felt Bill Clinton had some flaws, but he sure could make a damned good speech.

When George Bush questioned Clinton's right to be president because he had protested the war in Vietnam, I felt, "Shit! There were a whole lot of us who protested a bad war. Does that make us less worthy to be 'good Americans'?"

I volunteered to sing and hold a crowd for Clinton as he swung through Texas on the last day of campaigning before the election, first in San Antonio and later that night in Fort Worth. Governor Ann Richards hosted the afternoon rally in San Antonio. Clinton was running late.

I knew Ann pretty well and had played for her inauguration in '91. I asked her at the San Antonio rally if she thought some new lines to "Redneck Mother" would work and be appropriate.

Ann said, "Go for it. It'll loosen things up."
So on the flight to Fort Worth I wrote:

Up against the wall Republican President.
Your time in the White House has come and gone,
It's time we had a Democrat in that office,
Tomorrow let's vote in Bill and move along.
Now Bush has promised us no more new taxes

He has even said, "Now read my lips."
I've been sweet-talked a lot and learned my lesson
Before I get screwed I want to be kissed.

That night, about 6,000 people waited at the Fort Worth airport, Meacham Field. To keep people from leaving, I played for about an hour, between 11 p.m. and midnight, and I rehearsed the crowd to sing the new chorus.

Finally the plane touched down and out came the entourage: Bill and Hillary Clinton, Ann Richards, tons of photographers. They hit the stage and the crowd went crazy. Bill waved a hello to the crowd and thanked me for playing to keep everyone happy. He made a short speech (he'd just about lost his voice by now) and was going to walk along the front row and press the flesh.

Bill asked if I would sing one more while he went to shake some hands. Before he left the stage, I told the audience, "Let's show the future president how well we can sing together," and we swung into "Up Against The Wall Republican President."

The press corps loved it. One photographer said, "It's usually dull. You made it fun for once."

I guess that's how I got invited to play the inaugural ball in Washington when Clinton was elected.

The real cool part came after Clinton and Gore had been in office about a month. The band and I had a gig at the Birchmere, a little joint in Alexandria, Virginia, 250 people capacity and a favorite "listening room" of mine right across the Potomac from D.C. We got word during sound check that Vice President Gore was coming to the show that night and President Clinton wanted to come, too.

About half an hour before we went on, the backstage was crawling with Secret Service. They told me, "Keep it quiet. He'll come in the back way during your second song."

I said OK, we'd do "The Pickup Truck Song" as the second song.

We ended our opening song; everyone applauded. We started "The Pickup Truck Song," and through the kitchen door came Hillary and Bill with Tipper and Al.

While we played, heads were turning and everyone was mumbling.

Cosmic Bob Livingston, ever-present in the moment, said over the P.A., "Ladies and gentlemen, the President of the United States."

The whole place stood and applauded. Now I had to gather this crowd back to the performance. So I said, "Hey, why doesn't everybody just relax and let Bill and Al and their friends drink a beer and enjoy a regular night out?"

And that's pretty much what happened.

At one point, Bill and Hillary held hands and hugged each other when I sang "Woman In Texas," dedicated to my wife.

They all came backstage after the show, and we schmoozed for a while.

In 1996 the president asked me to come to South Dakota on the Monday night before Election Day. As I had done in '92, he wanted me to play his last rally before Election Day.

I was a good luck charm, he said.

Ron Crosby from Oneonta would never turn down a presidential invitation like that, and neither did Jerry Jeff Walker. It was a long flight, and a great night.

*   *   *

We continued to cut albums.

In 1992 we did *Hill Country Rain* at Cedar Creek Studios in Austin, co-produced with Lloyd Maines.

In 1993 we took a mobile truck to Luckenbach and brought together some the same people who had helped make *Viva Terlingua* twenty years earlier. Susan and I planned it as a love letter, a remembrance of the happy times we had spent in this quaint hill country town.

Becky Crouch, Hondo's daughter, read some of Hondo's writing, and I did a song I made up for Hondo years ago about Luckenbach, "Viva Luckenbach."

That's what we titled the album.

Viva Luckenbach!

There's a place I know where we all go
A little ways down the road
Ain't far from here, we like to sit and drink beer, play dominoes and tell jokes.
We've been stoppin' by since forty-nine, eighteen hundred I mean
Ain't nothin' fancy just kids and ranchers in clean white shirts and jeans.

CHORUS
> *You'll see lots of smilin' faces*
> *Little children runnin' around*
> *Everybody's somebody in an old Hill Country town*
> *Dirt daubers hummin' see sticker burrs on your socks*
> *Sure signs you spent some time in beautiful Luckenbach.*

Let me tell you now about the town
And how it came to be
In the eighteen hundreds
They came in buggies
To meet and trade and buy feed

They built a blacksmith shop
And then later on they added
The cotton gin, but the old dance hall
And general store is where it all begins and ends.

(Repeat Chorus)

In the fifties people moved to cities
Leaving it all behind
Luckenbach closed down for good
And just fell on harder times.

One day Hondo driving by
Wished he had a beer

So he bought the place and opened it up
And that's the reason we're all here

(Repeat Chorus twice)

It included a song about my grandmother Jessie giving me my first guitar, "The Gift."
"Gonzo Compadres" is a song the band and I made up on the road — silly business. My
favorite is Django's song, "Little Man."

Little Man

Hey, little man, you're quite a man
You make me smile when no one can
And days when I don't give a damn
You come and you take my hand
And we go walking a long, long way
Seeing what we'll see
Doin' things that can make me smile
When you do things that remind me of me

Hey, little man, understand
Your daddy's ain't nothing but a guitar man
Living his life the best he can
Till you came I hadn't a plan
But I've been walking a long, long way
And there are things I have seen
I learned things that might help you, son
When you do things that remind me of me.

BRIDGE:
  And you've got your own life to live, it's true
  And I just want the best in this life for you
  There are heartaches I could help you through
  If you want me to,
  But if I know you, you won't ask me to.

Hey, little man, you got to take a stand
Make up your mind to be all you can
Have a lot of pride and remember that
You're the son of a gypsy songman
When you're walking your long, long way
Seeing what you'll see
Looking back, won't you tip your hat
When you do things that remind you of me.

But hey, little man, now you take my hand
Walk a little way with your old man
It won't be long before you lead a band
And I'm just one of your fans
And when you're walking a long, long way
Seein' what you'll see
Remember people will smile sometimes
When you do things that remind them of me.

The title cut was a song I started making up for Hondo's pleasure back in '73, but I had never finished it. As a salute to Hondo, I finished it for the album; we've had a lot of fun with it since. Becky Crouch told me, "You captured the whole story in the one little song. It's so perfect." That's when it's fun being a songwriter.

Next we decided to make a Christmas album, with the kind of songs you want to put on and listen to when you're drinking a little wine and decorating the tree. Done our way, of course.

It was Susan's idea, and as usual it not only worked out well but turned into a lot of fun.

We had to start in May to ready it for fall release, so that it would sell before Christmas. We decorated a tree, cooked turkey and dressing in the kitchen, exchanged a few gifts, and sang our favorite Christmas songs. We went back to Cedar Creek Studio and finished up the album the next week, wearing shorts. We called it *Christmas Gonzo Style*.

*   *   *

One constant over the years has been my periodic yearning to travel for sheer pleasure, kick back and break the routine in some warm and enjoyable place. I've never outgrown the feeling of freedom I felt the first time I hitchhiked out of the Oneonta winter and stood a few days later on the warm beach at Fort Lauderdale with the sand between my toes.

Sweet escape!

Ever since Susan started managing my career, we had been conscious of trying to stay close to the fans, keep them informed of what I was doing and making them feel that they were a part of my music and my life . . . because they are.

In '93 we decided to combine this with my getaway impulse, and we hosted a Caribbean cruise with my fans.

I had hoped we could have a whole boat to ourselves, but we got mixed in with another group. We made the best of it by taking the last seating at dinner and taking over the back lounge from 10 p.m. until one o'clock in the morning.

It was horrible. All those cruise ships stop at the same places, and the ports are set up to gouge you when you dock — another case of the American lifestyle being over-the-top.

We must be a sight in Third World ports, consuming knickknack shit by the truckload, keeping the local people busy creating useless junk to sell to tourists who are floating around aimlessly in huge tubs of steel, gorging themselves the whole way.

As you can see, I didn't exactly enjoy my one and only cruise trip.

The cruise did tell me where I didn't want to be, and I began a search for some place relatively primitive, two hours from Texas, where they speak English.

In the fall of '93, after we released *Viva Luckenbach*, we made a trip to Aspen and met Brownie Rice. Browne Rice III had started a little resort on Ambergris Caye, a small island off Belize. The main community on the island is San Pedro, a town with sand streets where heavy traffic is just a rusty old golf cart creeping along. The Victoria House, which Brownie started, had only thirty-four rooms. We landed on a little airstrip where you literally pick up your bags and walk to the resort.

We liked it so much, we decided that we would use the resort for a get-together with some of our fans, the kind of thing we'd had in mind with the cruise the previous winter. Mid-January would be a good time to escape the winter, and we were sure our fans could fill the little resort.

We wanted it understood that we were going to have fun. The resort hadn't had a group like ours in a long time — maybe ever, come to think of it — but Brownie was up for it. We slept late. Fished in the afternoon. I sang after dinner and we partied till first light. The fishing guides may not have made much money, but the bartenders sure did.

It was great fun. Susan and I were captivated by the place and the people, a Mayan and Spanish mix. The population is 95 percent literate and English is the first language. They love their part of the world.

One reason it's so charming and beautiful is because the coastline is protected by 185 miles of coral reef. No "Love Boats" can get through — water's too shallow. The government has chosen to rely on visitors more inclined to the rustic. Not many man-made thrills, just pure nature. Let the natural beauty be your vacation.

They have large farms on the mainland where they grow vegetables, and you catch fresh fish from the sea. Coconuts and palm trees everywhere. Tropical breezes keep the temperature constant and pleasant. The town of San Pedro is owned and run by the old families. They're not in a big hurry to be like Americans.

San Pedro has some conveniences without losing the charm. It's not Cancun or Cozumel. They know they have a good life in a simple way. They are changing but not very rapidly. They are proud people and work hard, but take enough time to enjoy their "Isla Bonita." When you go to town at night, you're in *their* town.

They are a lovely people who only ask you to take them as they are. They love country music. Hey, it's only two hours from Texas.

Susan and I felt at home immediately. We decided to look for some land. A walk down the beach and, boom, we ran into a sign tacked to a tree that said to call Ramon Nuñez about prices.

Ramon, it turned out, was the unofficial mayor of San Pedro. Ramon was El Jefe, the man to see about anything that needed official sanction. He worked out the deal between the owner and us, and just like that, we became landowners in Belize!

Through Ramon we met Armando Graniel, the local contractor, and we discussed how to build a house and a boat dock.

Comfortable temperatures and pleasant breezes make it so relaxing. We have outdoor showers, go barefoot and dress as casually as possible.

I don't think I'm as happy anywhere else as there.

My penchant for fucking off really surfaces in Belize, but Susan is not one to let me "fish my life away." She keeps dreaming up new projects, or I'll mention something in passing and the next thing I know, I'm off to Europe or doing a new album because it's Christmas, and I don't have a Christmas album.

* * *

We continued to make music and cut albums.

I noticed a lot of college kids and other new faces were coming to shows, and I thought that we should put most of the songs that make up the meat of our set onto one album.

That became the idea for *Night After Night*: all the songs people like and sing along with, all the hits from over the years, but mostly in the way you've heard 'em at a live show somewhere.

They're all there. The ones we do night after night. Live, of course, and recorded over three nights with audiences at the Birchmere in Alexandria, Virginia.

I also did a songbook of those songs. That songbook showed in depth how I play them, and it served its purpose. More work than it's worth — my stuff isn't that complicated. It was a one-time thing, just like this book. But compared to writing this book, the songbook was a piece of cake.

We released the songbook and the album in '95, the year my grandmother, Jessie, turned 100. That was also the year I got my home site on the World Wide Web:

www.jerryjeff.com

The Web site was another of Susan's ideas, and one more example of her forward thinking. Had we waited another year or two, that domain name would've been gone for sure.

In 1996, I had some bits and pieces of songs and was leaning toward doing an album in Belize. As far as I knew, no artist had ever cut an album in Central America, which was enough to make me want to do it. That, and the fact that I knew it would be fun.

Susan dangled a compromise: "Go to Belize and write all original material for a studio album and the next one can be the beach thing you want to do." I jumped at that!

I spent ten days in April down in Belize and wrote all the tunes for *Scamp*.

It turned into one of our best projects: lots of airplay on Americana stations and some of the best stuff I'd written in a long time. Two of the songs came out of a sponsorship arrangement I've had with Miller Beer — "Down In Texas (Life Is Good)" and "Life On the Road," which was the result of twenty-five dates scheduled around Texas where we played as many old, funky, family-owned honky-tonks as we could find.

Definitely a Gonzo experience. London and Paris (Texas), through the Big Bend and back out through South Texas. Like many of my albums, *Scamp* is a reflection of my life during the period when I was creating it, from the honky-tonk tour songs to "Manny's Hat Song" to the boat dock in Belize.

We cut it at a studio in Austin, with Lloyd Maines again producing, and we released it in October of '96, not long after the tenth anniversary of Tried & True Music. It was my first album of all-original material since *Driftin' Way of Life* back in '69, and our best-received project since *Live At Gruene Hall* (unless you count my mother's endorsement of *Christmas Gonzo Style*).

We were very professional about our approach to making it: rehearsal, basic tracks, overdubs and harmonies. Just like the big boys do it. I can do that, but I don't have nearly as many memories as the live recordings give me.

Unlike many of the people I worked with in the business earlier in my career, my current manager always keeps her promises. With *Scamp* out of the way, I had the green light from management to do my Belize album.

Django began joining the old man onstage in 1999. This was taken at our annual Birthday Weekend concert at the Paramount Theatre in Austin . . . I wonder if one day I'll have to ask to be on his guest list.

After coming off a successful project like *Scamp*, I wondered whether I should take a bunch of digital equipment and go to a Third World country that barely has electricity so that I could make a follow-up album.

Then I thought, "But I've earned it. It's my reward."

I knew that something relaxing and fun would come out of a place so charming . . . like going to Luckenbach or Gruene Hall. We would have a good time, and it would show up on the record.

Recording live in Ambergris Caye would present some special problems that I tried to anticipate.

We rehearsed at my house in Austin. I told everybody — band members, recording engineer Charles Ray and Lloyd, who was producing — that everything we would need, we must take with us. So we rehearsed that way. If we couldn't carry it into the rehearsal room with us, we couldn't count on it.

We rehearsed in a room of the house where electrical outlets are not grounded, since that's what we'd be facing down in Belize. We kept the arrangements and the instrumentation as simple as possible. Any overdubs, we'd have to do back home.

I headed for Ambergris Caye a few days early. Among other details, I suspected a bad transformer on the utility pole outside my house. As soon as I got there, I called the Belize Electric Company, "Could someone come and look at my transformer? I have important work, and I must make sure it's right."

"Right away," the voice said.

In Belize everybody says "right away," and "right away" has grown to mean sometime between from this moment in time to possibly never. He might drive right over, or he might come next month.

I decided to drive by the office in my pickup truck. I found someone in charge and he rode with me to inspect the transformer.

From the ground he took one look up at the square box and said, "That one is about twenty years old, left here by the British. We are phasing them out."

"Could I get a new one?"

"Right away."

I told him, "If you send a crew down tomorrow I'll tip them and buy them a case of Belikan Beer."

"Sure thing."

They didn't come that Friday, they didn't work over the weekend, and the band was due on Monday. That morning, I got a call that the electric company crew was coming with the new transformer.

They got there a little after noon, two little guys and one big guy in a golf cart, and turned off all the power to the house.

It was hot and still in August, some breeze, but not much on that side of the house. The band was going to show up real soon, and this was my brilliant idea. I would look real bad if they walked into a house without electricity for the ceiling fans, much less for amps and recording equipment.

Outside, the big guy had climbed the pole and was handing stuff down to the two little guys.

I appeared occasionally with cold beers which the two guys on the ground drank. I wanted to keep the guy on the pole up there till he was finished. I knew if he came down for any reason and left, I might not see him for a week.

I brought a dozen cold beers out in a cooler.

"If you finish the job this afternoon, these are all for the man on the pole."

He looked down at me and at the open cooler and said, "It's almost done. I have to check the voltage."

I waited a little while and wandered back outside.

The big guy, still up on the pole, said, "I've got 110. I could give you 115."

"Sure, do it man."

I looked down toward the beach, and the boys were pulling up to the dock in the boat driven by our caretaker, Armando. As I was watching them unload and start walking up the boat dock, I saw the ceiling fans in the house start to turn.

I looked back at the crew from the electric company, and they were sitting on the cart drinking beer and smiling at me.

I smiled back and walked into the cool house to greet the boys.

We had discussed the fact that we weren't going to do a lot of "Yellow Bird" type songs with steel drums and bongos. We were going to play songs that dealt with things you'd experience in Belize.

I'd written "Come Away To Belize With Me," a song about a day in San Pedro, and "Cowboy Boots & Bathin' Suits" about packing up and going home to reality.

The rest of the songs were about the wind, rain, coconut trees and the moon.

"Barefootin'" because you go barefoot a lot; "Listen To The Fallin' Rain" because it's so nice to hear an afternoon shower on the roof.

Bill and Billie Courtney, two of our favorite people who were down once fishing with us, celebrated their anniversary in Belize one night. I sang them "The Moon Is Still Over Her Shoulder." Bill looked at all of us afterward and smiled and said, "Yeah, it still is."

Magic moment, and I knew it had to be on the record.

The Fred Neil medley was something I had wanted to do since 1968. It felt wonderful to do it in my house in Belize. There is no finer singer anywhere than Fred Neil. I've only had the pleasure to hear bits and pieces whenever Freddie passed through, but I listen to the CDs all the time.

My car CD player only has Chet Baker and Fred Neil (and occasionally the Mills Brothers).

The *Cowboy Boots & Bathin' Suits* CD was the most fun to make because there was no pressure, and I knew after all the other projects, it would come out OK.

So I just let it happen.

*　　*　　*

In 1994, we left the house in Oak Hill. Our kids were going to high school in Austin, and suburban sprawl had made the drive into town a nightmare. For a real vision of hell, try driving Interstate 35 through Austin during working hours. Or, better yet, just take my word for it, because I-35 through Austin does not need any more traffic.

We found a house in town, in an old neighborhood, a place with room for us and for our business offices.

Living in Austin, kicking back in Belize . . . about the only way life could be more delicious would be to have a place in the French Quarter.

And that's what we did.

Susan arranged for me to go on a Quarter search with a real estate agent named Eleanor Farnsworth. I had played Tipitina's the night before. When Eleanor knocked at my door at eleven the next morning I was still out. I suggested she go for Bloody Marys while I showered, and shortly thereafter, we were off.

I loved going into the old courtyards and seeing what was behind the front walls. We wound up looking at residential property that cost about three times what we had set out to spend, but I felt we should have something we loved, something that would bring us down often for visits; otherwise, we would probably only use it now and then.

We bought a nice house and the connecting double-shotgun cottage on St. Ann Street.

We flew to New Orleans to close on the deal and then spent the night in our new house. To pass the time while we were loading in the furniture, I picked up some CDs at the Quarter Music Store. Louis Armstrong, Mose Allison, Nina Simone, Bill Evans and an old favorite of mine, *Chet Baker Sings*.

The next morning — our first in the new place — I called the real estate agent who helped with the closing. I wanted to take him to lunch. He said, "OK, but stop around the corner. A new place on Burgundy Street came on the market today, and you should see it."

Susan and I walked over, enjoying the Quarter, and as we entered the house, I could see straight through to a courtyard with a swimming pool and a big magnolia tree. Along the left side of the living room was a wall of bookcases leading to French doors that opened onto the courtyard. High ceilings, and on the other side a huge master bedroom and bath.

I was smitten. I felt like this was where I was supposed to be. I walked around in a daze.

The next morning I sat on the edge of the bed in the house on St. Ann, staring out the window.

Susan asked, "Are you still thinking about that house we saw yesterday?"

I said, "It's so perfect, but I'll be OK here."

Da boys in da band, circa 1995 : left to right Bob Livingston, my ownself, Steady Freddie Krc, John Inmon.

She said, "Let's walk back over and look one more time."

That did it. We both concluded that the Burgundy Street house was better. We made an offer.

The owner of the Burgundy Street house took the offer but needed two months to get out. We needed two months to sell the properties we had just bought on St. Ann. Both houses dominoed, and we wound up where we wanted to be.

So here I sit in the French Quarter, surrounded by books, drawings of Babe Stovall, listening to Chet Baker. I have an old guitar in the corner and I'm writing about the journey from New Orleans street singer to homeowner. The house sits eight to ten blocks from the First Precinct jail where I met Bojangles.

The Quarter has remained about the same in many respects. The people are still friendly with a live-and-let-live attitude. Lots of unique characters: Johnny Donnels the photographer, gallery owner Marguerite Bergen, Herman Leonard the jazz photographer, and all the crew of Nola and Emeril's restaurants.

The street scene is busier that ever; lots of music everywhere.

I'd always heard that the music business could break your heart. It has a couple of times, but also I've been pretty lucky.

I started as a happy-go-lucky street singer, and the joy of playing and paying my way with music has held me in good stead.

I learned to love the craft of songwriting first. Afterwards, I'd found out that nobody else in the business knew any more than I did about making music. It was all up for grabs.

I could have taken a more commercial route, but I hated dissecting music and trying to make it fit a formula. I'm most comfortable with good musicians who listen to the lyrics and try to play what suits the story best.

I guess drinking gave me the courage to plow ahead with whatever it was I wanted to do.

Instinctively I was following my gut feeling.

Writing this book has been a sobering experience. In fact I've given up drinking to finish it. My pal Walter Hagen in Dallas said to me the other day, "You certainly had your share."

I answered back, "And a couple of other peoples' share, too."

I realized, as I was writing this book, that change was the one constant through much of my life. Change, sometimes in the form of upheaval and sudden separation, sometimes change for its own sake. Change for me was about finding freedom and independence, creating the room I needed to do what I wanted to do at the time, the way I wanted to do it. It isn't always pretty, but if you think you've got something special, the time will come when you have to stop being a nice guy and just go out and prove it.

I've probably only told half the tales, but this looks like it's the only book I'm ever going to write. You can carve that in stone. I've got too many songs to sing, and being a Gypsy Songman is what I'm best at.

Until I knock on your door,

Jerry Jeff

Layin' My Life On The Line

REFRAIN:
I know there's people who just sing
What they do is a whole different thing
But it's more than a business
If you stand as a witness
And lay your whole life on the line

So I'm laying my life on the line
That's what I do all the time
I find myself each night
Face in a white light
Layin' my life on the line.

Drivin' the road here tonight
My thoughts were of Susan and I
How her love sustained me
When the road almost claimed me
And laid my life out in a line.

Music is my way of life
And the travelin' gets crazy sometimes
Still it takes me places
Where I see the faces
Of people I touch with my lines.

BRIDGE:

Sometimes it all feels so right
Sometimes I feel far from home
Sometimes I wonder where am I headed
Have I been on this road for too long.

But here I am out here tonight
Playin' the songs that I like
'Cause the magic in singing
Comes through when you're bringing
Your whole life laid out in lines.

And I'm layin' my life on the line.